Dictionary
of Bibliometrics

Dictionary of Bibliometrics

Virgil Diodato, PhD

Routledge
Taylor & Francis Group
New York   London

First published by

The Haworth Press, Inc., 10 Alice Street, Binghamton, NY 13904-1580

This edition published 2012 by Routledge

Routledge
Taylor & Francis Group
711 Third Avenue
New York, NY 10017

Routledge
Taylor & Francis Group
2 Park Square, Milton Park
Abingdon, Oxon OX14 4RN

Library of Congress Cataloging-in-Publication Data

Diodato, Virgil Pasquale, 1945-
    Dictionary of bibliometrics / Virgil Diodato.
       p.   cm.
    Includes bibliographical references and index.
    ISBN 1-56024-852-1 (acid free paper).
    1. Bibliometrics–Dictionaries. I. Title.
Z669.8.D56 1994
020′.3–dc20

93-3952
CIP

CONTENTS

ABOUT THE AUTHOR

Virgil Diodato, MA, MLS, PhD, is Associate Professor at the University of Wisconsin–Milwaukee, School of Library and Information Science, where he teaches courses in bibliometrics, indexing, and the foundations of information science. He has written more than forty articles on these topics and others and is co-author of the *Business Information Desk Reference*. Dr. Diodato has been at the University of Wisconsin–Milwaukee since 1981, but interrupted his service from 1985-1988 to become Assistant Director for Public Services at Governors State University Library. A member of the American Society for Information Science and the American Society of Indexers, he volunteers some of his time every week to staff the reference desk of Cardinal Stritch College Library in Milwaukee.

Preface

Bibliometrics is a field that uses mathematical and statistical techniques, from counting to calculus, to study publishing and communication patterns in the distribution of information.

Bibliometrics even appears in the daily newspaper. A recent article in *The New York Times* had this headline: "Ranking Law Schools by Faculty Publishing Rate." The article discussed a new way to evaluate law schools. The old way asked the opinion of judges, law school deans, and attorneys. The new way counts how many pages each faculty member in the law school publishes over a five year period. That is one of many bibliometric techniques (Ranking Law Schools, 1992).

PURPOSE OF THE DICTIONARY

This dictionary explains some 225 terms used in bibliometrics. Its first purpose is to give the reader nontechnical definitions of bibliometric concepts. Although most definitions are brief, they provide enough information to verify the meaning of a term and to lead the reader to other related terms. The second purpose of the dictionary is to suggest sources where the reader can find more information about the defined term.

The definitions should help the reader who needs to remember or verify a bibliometric concept used before. For example, definitions of bibliographic coupling and cocitation help distinguish these commonly confused concepts. The definitions should also help the reader who needs to find out about a new concept. For example, someone taking on a study of obsolescence for the first time can use the dictionary to discover the various types of obsolescence and brief descriptions of how they are measured.

AUDIENCE

This dictionary is for users of bibliometrics, whether they are librarians, information scientists, or subject specialists.

Librarians employ bibliometrics in some evaluations of their collections. For example, a librarian may do a citation analysis or a Bradford analysis to evaluate a periodical collection.

Some information scientists, especially bibliometricians, study the theoretical aspects of bibliometric laws and techniques. A bibliometrician may test the applicability of Bradford's law and Lotka's law to the study of certain subject fields.

Subject specialists outside of library and information science employ bibliometrics to analyze their own subject fields. Chemists, historians, musicians, and people in many other fields use bibliometrics to identify communication patterns and to answer questions like: Who cites whom? What are the hot topics in our field? Which institutions are the most productive or scholarly?

SCOPE: BIBLIOMETRICS; INFORMETRICS; SCIENTOMETRICS

Should bibliometrics be called bibliometrics? Or should it be called informetrics or scientometrics? There is disagreement about this. I feel that bibliometrics is a kind of informetrics and that scientometrics, in turn, is a type of bibliometrics. Others will disagree. So, when the dictionary uses the term "bibliometrics," some readers may want to substitute "informetrics" or "scientometrics."

The reader may want to look at the entries in the dictionary for these three terms and note the variety of overlapping meanings.

Bibliometrics

Bibliometrics may be the most commonly used of the three terms. Therefore, when there has been a choice, this dictionary has emphasized bibliometrics over informetrics and scientometrics.

Bibliometrics has been used during the past quarter of a century to refer to mathematical and statistical analyses of patterns that arise in the publication and use of documents. Even people new to the field may have heard of bibliometric concepts such as Bradford's law, citation analysis, and publication counts.

Publications or documents (this dictionary tends to use the word "documents") can be thought of broadly and need not be confined to items that appear in paper. Bibliometrics can cover analyses of electronic journals, voice mail, and video images.

Informetrics

Informetrics is sometimes used synonymously with bibliometrics. However, a good distinction can be made. Informetrics examines patterns that show up not only in publications but also in many aspects of life, as long as the patterns deal with information. Therefore, informetrics can be viewed as a general term that includes bibliometrics, and perhaps also all of scientometrics.

For example, Bradford's law is more bibliometric than informetric. This law refers, in part, to the tendency for relatively few sources, such as particular journals, to be the most prolific producers of materials in a given field. On the other hand, Willis' law rests much more in informetrics than in bibliometrics. It deals with the relationship between the age of a species of plant or animal and the area that the species inhabits. What does such a law have to do with information? To botanists, Willis' law provides information about patterns of plant and animal habitations. But more importantly to informetricians, the concepts, formulas, and graphs that Willis described can be applied to the analysis of other entities, including publication patterns.

This dictionary covers informetrics when it overlaps with bibliometrics. There is little coverage of the technical mathematical models that are often associated with informetrics.

Scientometrics

Scientometrics applies bibliometric techniques to science. Science here refers to the physical and natural sciences, and mathematics, but does not usually include the social sciences. An example of both bibliometrics and scientometrics would be a study of how often and in what situations astronomers write articles that include references to physicists.

Scientometrics often goes beyond usual bibliometric techniques, as when scientometrics examines the development and even the politics of the sciences. Therefore, scientometrics can compare science research policies from country to country or the amount of money or number of scientists in each nation. In this dictionary, coverage of scientometrics emphasizes the areas where it overlaps with bibliometrics.

SCOPE: SCHOLARLY COMMUNICATION; EVALUATION OF INFORMATION SERVICES

The dictionary contains some terms from two other areas: (1) scholarly communication, and (2) the evaluation of information services.

Scholarly Communication

Scholarly communication examines how scholars, scientists, and other professionals communicate with each other. Only some of the concepts and techniques of this field are covered in the dictionary, especially when they overlap with bibliometrics. One instance of overlap is the study of citations, which offers evidence of communication among scholars.

Evaluation of Information Services

Librarians and others evaluate the effectiveness and efficiency of their information services. For example, for the analysis of a periodical collection, the dictionary has many terms that deal with citations and with Bradford's law. However, the dictionary does not cover terms in areas such as budgeting and surveys of users.

SELECTION OF TERMS

The selection of terms has been subjective. The goal has been to select many of the best known or most recently used terms that would be sought by today's users of bibliometrics.

SPECIAL FEATURES

A typical entry contains a definition and one or more sample references. There are also cross references and an index.

Sample References

If the reader needs more information than the definition provides for a term, the *sample reference(s)* may be helpful.

The *sample reference* is usually a recent (1988-1992) article by a user of the technique or concept that is defined. The recent *sample references* are not necessarily the best articles on the given topics nor are they all authored by the most well-known authors in the field. However, they are recent. There is a heavy emphasis on the major sources of bibliometric articles, including: *Journal of Documentation; Journal of Information Science; Journal of the American Society for Information Science*; and *Scientometrics*.

Some *sample references* are old. A few are decades old. Sometimes an old reference written by the originator of a term provides the best explanation of the term. Nevertheless, this is not a dictionary of etymology. Most of the *sample references* are recent and do not indicate where the term originated.

The interpretations of the content of the *sample references* are my own. Many of the *sample references* make their points so well that the dictionary includes direct quotes from them.

Full bibliographic data for the *sample references* are listed at the end of the dictionary, after the Z's.

Cross References

See references lead the reader from one version of a term to another version. An example is: ·

sources and items. *See* **items and sources.**

Comparisons appear in bold after the phrase "Compare with" and lead the reader to related terms. For example, in the definition for acknowledgement . . . Compare with **peer interactive communication.**

Opposing terms appear within parentheses and in italics after the phrase "opposed to." For example, in the definition for

allocitation. A citation from one document to another such that there is no self citation (opposed to *autocitation*) . . . .

A hidden entry appears within parentheses and in bold and directs the reader to another definition of interest. For example, in the definition for

adjusted count . . . This is an issue when one is analyzing publications with multiple authors **(authorship, multiple)** . . .

Variants

A synonymous word for the defined term appears in bold after the phrase "Also called." For example, in the definition for

author, primary . . . Also called **first author, senior author** . . . .

Index of Names

Because names are so important in bibliometrics (Barnaby Rich effect, Lotka's law, Price's index), the Index of Names covers the occurrence of all personal names anywhere in the dictionary. It follows the list of Sample References at the end of the book.

MATHEMATICAL TERMINOLOGY AND SYMBOLS

The words "curve" and "line" are used synonymously in the descriptions of graphs.

In equations, two methods are used to indicate multiplication:

parentheses and the asterisk. For example, the following two expressions are the same:

3 (x + 1)
3 * (x + 1)

They both mean: 3 multiplied by (x plus 1).

QUOTES

A few of the quotes from the *sample references* contain italicized words. In every case, the emphasis is that of the author(s) of the *sample reference*.

A few quotes from the older *sample references* contain language that we would call sexist today. I have decided to leave the language as written by the authors rather than to hide the language with ellipses and bracketed rewordings.

ACKNOWLEDGEMENTS

Arts & Humanities Citation Index®, *Journal Citation Reports®*, *Science Citation Index®*, and *Social Sciences Citation Index®* are registered trademarks of the Institute for Scientific Information.

Thanks to Dr. Dietmar Wolfram, Dr. Helen Humeston, Stephan Mattsen, and Paul Schaleger for their comments and suggestions on earlier versions of this manuscript.

Virgil Diodato
Milwaukee, WI

REFERENCE

Ranking law schools by faculty publishing rate. (1992, July 17). *The New York Times*, p. B8.

A

acknowledgement. A personal expression of thanks to others that an author may place in his/her article or book. Compare with **peer interactive communication**.

In the *sample reference*, Cronin, McKenzie, and Stiffler (1992) analyze the acknowledgements appearing in 20 years of four library and information science journals. They test for a correlation between highly cited and highly acknowledged individuals.

adaption innovation theory. *See* **Kirton adaption innovation theory**.

adaptor. An individual who (1) modifies his/her usual activities by accepting or using a new or changed device or idea; or (2) tends not to innovate (and not to introduce new ideas to colleagues) but instead receives and uses new devices and ideas developed by others. Compare with **adopter, innovator**.

In the first sense, to be an adaptor may require also being an adopter. For example, if a historian accepts an electronic spreadsheet as a new way of recording data, the historian has adapted his/her activities by adopting the new method.

In the second sense, being an adaptor is seen as the opposite of being an innovator. For example, assume a historian accepts an electronic spreadsheet as a new way to record data. Where did the historian get this new idea? If historian A gets the idea from historian B, then historian A is an adaptor. Historian B is an innovator, if historian B thought of the idea and then shared it with historian A.

adjusted count. One way to determine how many documents a person has authored. This is an issue when one is analyzing publications with multiple authors (**authorship, multiple**). Compare with **complete count, straight count**.

For an example of an adjusted count, assume there are four documents with the following authors:

Document 1 is authored by Queen, Jack, and King;
Document 2 is authored by Jack;
Document 3 is authored by King and Queen.
Document 4 is authored by Jack and Jill.

When doing an adjusted count, the rule is to use fractions to distribute responsibility for multiple authorship. A common way to calculate each author's responsibility is to be sure that the tallies for all the authors of a single document always add up to 1. So, in Document 1 above, Queen, Jack, and King are each counted as 1/3. In Document 2, Jack is counted as 1. In Document 3, King and Queen are each counted as 1/2. In Document 4, Jack and Jill are each counted as 1/2. In summary:

Queen has $1/3 + 1/2 = 5/6$ of a publication;
Jack has $1/3 + 1 + 1/2 = 1\ 5/6$ publications;
King has $1/3 + 1/2 = 5/6$ of a publication;
Jill has 1/2 of a publication.

In the first *sample reference*, Lindsey (1980) suggests a method for doing an adjusted count and then compares adjusted and complete (or normal) counts of the same collection of documents.

In the second *sample reference*, Nicholls (1989) examines 30 studies of Lotka's law and indicates how each researcher counts authorship.

adopter. An individual who accepts or uses a new or changed device or idea. There can be many adopters for a single item. Therefore, an adopter is not usually the very first person to adopt, but the term is sometimes used to refer to the first group of people to become adopters over a specified period of time.

The concept is important in the study of how scholars, scientists, and professionals communicate with each other. For example, it is interesting to determine the characteristics of the first adopters of a new medical treatment, a new statistical tool, or a new phrase. Compare with **adaptor, innovator**.

In the *sample reference*, Messeri (1988) compares scientists' ages with their tendency to adopt or not adopt new theories in the field of plate tectonics.

advertising content. The type and number of advertisements found in a document.

In the *sample reference*, Kazlauskas, DeYoe, and Smith (1989) analyze advertisements in microcomputer periodicals.

affiliation. The organization or place of business with which an author is associated. Compare with **endogenous document, exogenous document**.

Analyses of affiliation can be used to evaluate or compare organizations or journals.

In the first *sample reference*, Herubel (1990) examines the affiliation of authors of articles, notes, and reviews that appear in the *Journal of the Society of Architectural Historians*.

In the second *sample reference*, Williamson (1989) reports on the occupation, gender, and geographic location of authors in five regional library journals.

age, citation. *See* **citation age; mean citation age; median citation age**.

age, human. A characteristic studied in scholarly communication and scientometrics. For example, one may examine: the correlation between age and research performance; the link between age and creativity; whether age is a factor in the Matthew effect; or if age affects how quickly a person becomes an adoptor of new methods and theories.

In the *sample reference*, Messeri (1988) studies the correlation between age and the adoption of new theories.

ageing or **aging**. *See* **obsolescence**.

allocitation. A citation from one document to another such that there is no self citation (opposed to *autocitation*). The two documents do not share a common author.

In the *sample reference*, van der Heij, van der Burg, Cressie, and Wedel (1990) introduce this term. See **autocitation** for a quote from their paper.

article cohort. *See* **Bradford article cohort**.

Arts & Humanities Citation Index®. A publication of the Institute for Scientific Information. In its citation index it indicates who cites whom, and so it can be a source of data for a citation analysis in the arts and humanities.

associativity. The mean number of authors per document in a group of documents. Compare with **author number**; **authorship, multiple**; **collaboration**.

If one subject area averages 2.5 authors per article and a second subject area averages 1.1 authors per article, then in some sense the authors in the first field associate with each other more than the authors in the second field.

In the *sample reference*, Chatelin and Arvanitis (1992) compare associativity with other **bibliometric indicators** of science activity in Cote d'Ivoire.

attraction power of a journal. The portion of articles that the journal publishes by authors outside the country, language, or organization usually associated with the journal. Compare with **exogenous documents**.

For example, if a journal is published in France and if there is no restriction on the language of publication, a 100 percent attraction rate for the journal means that all the articles are in languages other than French.

In the *sample reference*, Arvanitis and Chatelin (1988) study the attraction power of journals published in northern nations to authors who live in southern countries.

author cocitation analysis. *See* **cocitation analysis, author**.

author impact factor. *See* **impact factor, author**.

author number. The number of authors of a document. Compare with **associativity**; **authorship, multiple**; **collaboration**.

In the *sample reference*, White (1991) examines correlations between title sizes and author numbers of documents.

author, primary. Usually the author listed first on the title page of a document. If the document has only one author, then the author is considered the primary author. Also called **first author, senior author**. Compare with **author, secondary**.

"Primary" or "senior" may also indicate importance of an author rather than location of the author's name. In that case, one may need a method, perhaps by questionnaire or citation analysis, to determine which author is the most important. Some journals indicate the primary author by placing an asterisk or other symbol next to that person's name. The first author listed is not necessarily the one who is most important or the one who contributed most to the document. Authors may be listed alphabetically, by rank, by who needs the most visibility, and by other social factors.

In the *sample reference*, Long, McGinnis, and Allison (1980) compare two ways to count an individual's publications and citations. One method counts only the documents for which the individual is the primary author; the other method counts all of an individual's publications, regardless of his/her place as primary or secondary author. Compare with **adjusted count, complete count, straight count**.

author proportiometric index. A measure of an author's research performance based on the length of the author's publications and on the number of coauthors. The simplest version of this index for a given author and a given document is:

$$\frac{\text{number of pages in the document}}{\text{number of authors of the document}}$$

For example, the author proportiometric index is:

8.33 for each author, in a 25-page article with 3 authors;
5.00 for each author, in a 25-page article with 5 authors;
8.00 for each author, in a 40-page article with 5 authors;
40.00 for the sole author of a 40-page article.

In the *sample reference*, Trenchard (1992) introduces this measure and suggests an enhancement. The enhancement is a weight that depends on whether the author is the first, second, third, . . . author listed.

author, secondary. Any author other than the primary one (**author, primary**). Usually this means any author listed as the second, third, or subsequent name on the title page of the document. Also called **junior author**.

It is possible to call someone a secondary author because that person contributes relatively little to a publication, regardless of the listing of the authors' names. This usage of the term requires a method, like a questionnaire or citation analysis, to measure each author's contribution to the document.

authorship, multiple. An instance in which two or more individuals jointly author a document. In such a case, the author number of the document is greater than one. Multiple authorship is sometimes used synonymously with coauthorship, though some writers may prefer the term coauthorship for documents jointly authored by exactly two authors. Also called **coauthorship, collaboration**.

Associativity is another measure of the number of authors, but it is an average taken over many documents.

Counting how many documents an author has published is complicated if the author has participated in multiple authorships. In such cases, there are at least three ways to count authorship: **adjusted count, complete count**, and **straight count**.

In the first *sample reference*, Schubert and Braun (1992) examine documents in which multiple authorship is shared by authors representing two or more countries.

In the second *sample reference*, Narin (1991) examines the incidence of multiple authorship in Europe.

In the third *sample reference*, Williamson and Williamson (1989) study the frequency and gender of multiple authorship in five regional library journals.

autocentered document. A document that reports research done in a particular geographic area, such that the document is published in the same geographic area where the research was done.

In the *sample reference*, Arvanitis and Chatelin (1988) develop this measure to study the autonomy of national research in soil sciences. They say that an autocentered report of soil research must obey three conditions: "(i) the research is carried out by a national laboratory; (ii) it treats a local agricultural problem; (iii) it is published in a local review or book" (p. 124).

autocitation. A citation for which an individual is an author of both the citing document and the cited document (opposed to *allocitation*). Also called **self citation**.

In the *sample reference*, van der Heij, van der Burg, Cressie, and Wedel (1990) introduce the term and its antonym, allocitation. They say:

> We are aware of the neologistic nature of the terms "autocitations" and "allocitations." Garfield . . . and others use the term "self-citations," but we do not know of the opposite to that term. "Self-citations" and "allocitations" would be linguistically unrelated, and "non-self-citations" not very elegant. (p. 157)

B

Barnaby Rich effect. A hypocritical attitude toward overpublication. A person with this attitude decries unchecked growth of the primary literature (**literature, primary**) of a field while contributing to that very growth. It is named for writer and soldier Barnaby Rich (1542-1617), whose name is also spelled Barnabe Riche and many other ways.

In the *sample reference* Braun and Zsindely (1985) coin this term because they note that Rich was unhappy about " 'the multiplicity of books,' " and yet he wrote at least 26 himself (pp. 529-530). The writers say: "We feel the attitude *Rich* represents is a manifestation of a very common effect defined as 'it's always the other author(s) who publishes too much . . . , never me' " (p. 530).

behavioral bibliometrics. *See* **bibliometrics, behavioral**.

biased citation. *See* **citation, biased**.

bibliograph. To some, this is a graph of any curve (**Bradford curve**) that describes Bradford's law.

To others who work with Bradford's law, this is a particular graph: the cumulative number of items (usually articles) on the vertical axis versus the logarithm of the rank number of sources (usually journals) on the horizontal axis.

Exhibit 1a is an example of that particular graph. It is a bibliograph of Bradford's own data for articles and journals in applied geophysics. From the first *sample reference*, Bradford (1934) supplies data such as the following:

the top ranked journal produces 93 articles;
the top 2 journals together produce 179 articles;
the top 3 journals together produce 235 articles;
    and so on until
the top 108 journals together produce 1065 articles;

the top 157 journals together produce 1163 articles;
the top 326 journals together produce 1332 articles.

In Exhibit 1a, the vertical axis plots the article numbers 93, 179, 235, . . ., 1065, 1163, and 1332. The horizontal axis of the bibliograph plots the common logarithms of 1, 2, 3, . . ., 108, 157, and 326.

Some may prefer to say they are plotting the logarithm of the cumulative number of journals along the horizontal axis (rather than the logarithm of the ranks).

Curves like the ones in Exhibits 1a and 1b are sometimes called J-curves or S-curves, depending on their shapes. The curve in Exhibit 1a is closer to the shape of a J, while the curve in Exhibit 1b is closer to the shape of an S. The latter curve is based on hypothetical data that clearly show the S shape.

EXHIBIT 1a.
A bibliograph of Bradford's law.

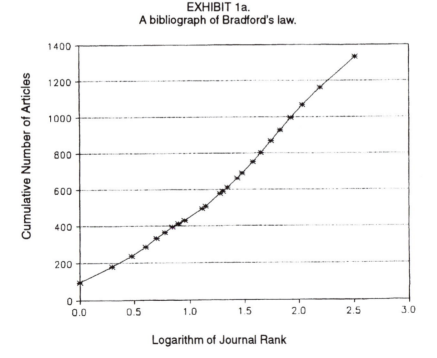

EXHIBIT 1b.
The S shape of a bibliograph.

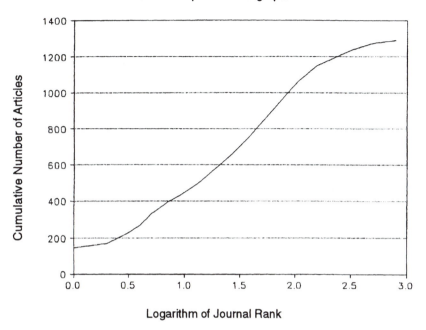

Logarithm of Journal Rank

Look at other graphs of data for Bradford's law in the entry for the **Bradford curve**.

In the second *sample reference*, Brooks (1990) notes at least one reason for the analysis of bibliographs: "[a] major expenditure of scholarly energy for the last two decades has been the modeling and identification of the slope of bibliographs" (p. 187).

bibliographic connectedness. Two documents are bibliographically connected if they are linked in one or more of the following ways: they share the same author; they have an indexing term or important title word in common; they are articles in the same journal; they cite each other (**citations, mutual**); they are simultaneously cited (**cocitation**) by a third document; they have at least one citation in common in their lists of references (**bibliographic coupling**).

You have to decide how far to take some of these relationships when considering if two documents are bibliographically connected. For example, if connectedness depends on the documents being in the same journal, do they have to be in the same issue? The same volume? Anywhere in the run of the journal?

The two connected documents should have enough in common to lead a reader of one to find the other.

In the *sample reference*, Swanson (1987) uses some of the factors listed above to note how two intellectually or logically related sets of documents in the medical literature are not bibliographically connected.

bibliographic coupling. The situation in which two documents each have citations to one or more of the same publications. The two citing documents are said to be coupled because if they cite the same publication(s), they may deal with similar subject matter. The strength of the coupling between the citing documents depends on the percent or number of total citations that they have in common.

Bibliographic coupling is related to cocitations. In Exhibit 2 let us say that:

document I cites documents A, B, C, and D;
document II cites documents C, D, E, F and G;

Therefore,

documents I and II are bibliographically coupled because
    they both cite documents C and D; documents I and II would
    still be bibliographically coupled even if they had only docu-
    ment C in common;
also, many pairs of documents are cocited; for example,
    documents E and F are cocited (by document II);
    documents D and E are cocited (by document II);
    documents A and B are cocited (by document I);
    documents C and D are cocited (by document I and by docu-
    ment II).

In the *sample reference*, Robinson (1991) suggests that bibliographic coupling between an unpublished manuscript and articles in

EXHIBIT 2.
Bibliographically coupled and cocited documents.

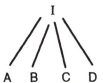

journals may be a way to identify the most appropriate journals for submission of the manuscript.

bibliographic data. The author, title, place of publication, and other such information about a document. Also called **bibliographic information**.

bibliographic information. *See* **bibliographic data**.

bibliograph slope. *See* **slope, bibliograph**.

bibliometric indicator. A measure that provides information about the nature of a subject field. Compare with **citation**; **cocitation**; **citation type**; **immediacy index**; **impact factor**; and **obsolescence**.

For scientific subject fields, also called **science indicator**.

In the *sample reference*, King (1987) examines the role of the indicators in the evaluation of research.

bibliometric reconstruction. *See* **reconstruction**.

bibliometrics. The main subject of this dictionary. A few writers call the field bibliometry. Bibliometrics used to be called **statistical bibliography**.

Sometimes bibliometrics and informetrics are used synonymously. Other times, bibliometrics is seen as a subfield within informetrics. In addition, bibliometrics overlaps with scientometrics.

The first two *sample references* give typical definitions of bibliometrics.

According to the first *sample reference*: "[Bibliometrics is t]he application of various statistical analyses to study patterns of authorship, publication, and literature use. . . ." (Lancaster, 1977, p. 353).

According to the second *sample reference*: "Bibliometrics is the quantitative study of literatures as they are reflected in bibliographies" (White and McCain, 1989, p. 119).

Major areas of bibliometric research include:

- bibliometric laws or distributions, such as Bradford's law, Lotka's law, and Zipf's law;
- citation analysis;
- indicators of research performance.

In the third *sample reference*, Egghe (1988a) labels the subdisciplines of bibliometrics as: statistics, operations research, bibliometric laws, citation analysis, circulation theory, information theory, and theoretical aspects of information retrieval.

The next five *sample references* provide historical information on the development of bibliometrics.

In the fourth *sample reference*, Narin (1991) says: "The first known example of bibliometric research is reported in an elegant paper published by Cole and Eales in 1917" (p. 34).

The fifth *sample reference* is the paper by Cole and Eales (1917) mentioned above. They title their work "A Statistical Analysis of the Literature" of comparative anatomy. The work includes charts of the literature from 1550 to 1860.

In the sixth *sample reference*, Pritchard (1969) recommends bibliometrics as a new name for what some had called statistical bibliography: "[I]t is suggested that a better name for this subject . . . is Bibliometrics, i.e. the application of mathematics and statistical methods to books and other media of communication" (p. 349).

According to the seventh *sample reference*, Pritchard was the apparent coiner of bibliometrics (Broadus, 1987).

Finally, the eighth *sample reference* (Prytherch, 1990) gives a library oriented definition: "[Bibliometrics is t]he application of mathematical and statistical methods to the study of the use made of books and other media within and between library systems" (p. 62).

bibliometrics, behavioral. An infrequently used expression for the analysis of relationships among documents.

In the *sample reference* Nicholas and Ritchie (1978) distinguish between behavioral bibliometrics and descriptive bibliometrics (**bibliometrics, descriptive**). They say that behavioral bibliometrics confirms that "[i]nside the literature there exists, in fact, a web of relationships." These relationships are usually caused by citations. So, citation analysis may be a synonym for behavioral bibliometrics (p. 10).

bibliometrics, descriptive. An infrequently used expression that refers to the collection of descriptive information about documents.

In the *sample reference*, Nicholas and Ritchie (1978) distinguish between descriptive bibliometrics and behavioral bibliometrics (**bibliometrics, behavioral**). The latter often involves the study of citations. On the other hand, descriptive bibliometrics collects information such as:

1. Bodies responsible for the production and transmission of the information.
2. Form of transmission (e.g., journal, monograph).
3. Medium of communication (e.g., article, letter).
4. Nature of information conveyed–subject and language characteristics.
5. Timing and frequency with which information is conveyed.
6. Amount of information conveyed.
7. Geographical origin. (p. 10)

bibliometry. *See* **bibliometrics**.

Booth's law. A revision of what some call Zipf's second law (**Zipf's law**). It is named for Andrew D. Booth.

In a given text, count the occurrences of all the different words. Rank the words so that the word having the most occurrences is given rank one. Booth's law is a mathematical description of the words at the bottom of the ranking list–the words that occur infrequently. (How infrequent this is depends on the text being analyzed, but it almost always refers to words occurring only once, twice, three, four, or five times each.)

As expressed by Booth (1967, p. 391) in the first *sample reference*, one version of Booth's law is:

$$\frac{I_n}{I_1} = \frac{2}{n(n + 1)}$$

where:

I_n is the number of words that occur n times each;
I_1 is the number of words that occur once each.

For example, if n = 4, then the equation above is:

$$\frac{I_4}{I_1} = \frac{2}{4(4 + 1)} = \frac{2}{20}$$

This predicts that the ratio of words occurring four times each to words occurring one time each is 2/20 or 0.10.

In the first *sample reference*, Booth (1967, p. 389) expresses Zipf's second law in a form that may be compared with Booth's revision. Zipf's second law is:

$$\frac{I_n}{I_1} = \frac{3}{4n^2 - 1}$$

In the second *sample reference*, Chen and Leimkuhler (1990) describe a modification of Booth's law.

boundary-spanning communication. See **communication, boundary-spanning**.

Bradford analysis. A means to: (1) test how well Bradford's law applies to a collection of items and sources (usually articles and journals); or (2) identify the core journals in a field.

To do a Bradford analysis for a given subject field and given time period:

- identify many or all items (usually articles) published in this field;

- list the sources (usually journals) that publish the articles (or items) in rank order beginning with the source that produces the most items;
- while retaining the order of the sources, divide this list into groups (or zones) so that the number of items produced by each group of sources is about the same.

For example, assume that a comprehensive search for articles on a certain topic over a given period of time identifies 200 journals that produce 1,520 articles. After ranking them, from most productive journals to least (in this subject area), they may divide into groups that look like this:

1st zone:　 10 journals that produce 505 articles;
2nd zone:　 22 journals that produce 495 articles;
3rd zone: 168 journals that produce 520 articles.

The ten top ranked journals are the core or most productive journals among the 200 journals examined.

In the *sample reference*, Wallace (1987) describes the basics of Bradford's law and its applications to libraries. These applications include analysis of the:

> literature of specific subjects, . . . productivity of monograph publishers, library circulation, . . . distribution of reference questions per requester, . . . distribution of users of journals, . . . distribution of journals for which photocopies are requested, ... (p. 44)

Bradford article cohort. The articles in a Bradford zone that one gathers during a Bradford analysis. The Bradford article cohort may refer to the group of articles themselves in a given zone or the number of articles in the zone. In the latter case, you can refer to "the" cohort for the analysis or "the size" of the cohort if the size is indeed about the same for each zone. Also called **article cohort, cohort**.

See the example in the definition for Bradford analysis. Using that example, the article cohort of the first zone is 505 articles.

Bradford curve. The graph that results from a test of Bradford's law. The Bradford curve shows a relationship between the number of articles on a given topic and the number of journals that produce the articles. Also called the **Bradford-Zipf curve**. Compare with **Zipf's law**.

For example, consider the first *sample reference*, in which Bradford (1934) himself analyzes applied geophysics (1928-1931). He finds 1,332 articles published in 326 journals. These data are listed cumulatively in columns A and B of Exhibit 3. For example, the most productive journal produces 93 articles on applied geophysics; the top two journals produce a total of 179 articles; the top 13 journals produce 493 articles; the top 20 journals produce 590 articles; and so on.

There are various ways to graph this data. That is why Exhibit 3 contains six columns.

Column A is the cumulative number of journals;
Column B is the corresponding cumulative number of articles;
Column C has the common logarithms of the data in Column A;
Column D has the common logarithms of the data in Column B;
Column E lists the percents of the data in Column A, with 326 journals corresponding to 100 percent;
Column F lists the percents of the data in Column B, with 1332 articles corresponding to 100 percent.

Then,

Exhibit 4a shows Column B versus Column A;
Exhibit 4b shows Column D versus Column C;
Exhibit 4c shows Column F versus Column E;
Exhibit 4d shows Column B versus Column C;

Exhibits 4a and 4c show the hyperbolic shape of Bradford's curve.

In Exhibit 4b, logarithms are used for the data on both axes. If logarithms are used only for the horizontal axis, as in Exhibit 4d, the graph is known as a semi-log graph; this results in what some call a bibliograph. Others refer to the semi-log result as the Bradford J-curve or S-curve. Compare with **Groos droop**.

The logarithmic examples here use common logarithms. The basic shapes of the examples would not change if natural logarithms were used instead.

EXHIBIT 3.
Data for a Bradford curve.

A	B	C	D	E	F
1	93	0	1.968	0.31	6.98
2	179	0.301	2.253	0.61	13.44
3	235	0.477	2.371	0.92	17.64
4	283	0.602	2.452	1.23	21.25
5	329	0.699	2.517	1.53	24.70
6	364	0.778	2.561	1.84	27.33
7	392	0.845	2.593	2.15	29.43
8	412	0.903	2.615	2.45	30.93
9	429	0.954	2.632	2.76	32.21
13	493	1.114	2.693	3.99	37.01
14	508	1.146	2.706	4.29	38.14
19	578	1.279	2.762	5.83	43.39
20	590	1.301	2.771	6.13	44.29
22	612	1.342	2.787	6.75	45.95
27	662	1.431	2.821	8.28	49.70
30	689	1.477	2.838	9.20	51.73
38	753	1.580	2.877	11.66	56.53
45	802	1.653	2.904	13.80	60.21
56	868	1.748	2.939	17.18	65.17
68	928	1.833	2.968	20.86	69.67
85	996	1.929	2.998	26.07	74.77
108	1065	2.033	3.027	33.13	79.95
157	1163	2.196	3.066	48.16	87.31
326	1332	2.513	3.125	100.00	100.00

In the second *sample reference*, Lancaster (1988) shows a picture of an ideal Bradford curve, noting that it applies not only to Bradford's law but also to other laws, including Zipf's law and Trueswell's 80/20 rule (pp. 34-35).

Bradford distribution. *See* **Bradford's law.**

Bradford factor. *See* **Bradford multiplier.**

Bradford group. *See* **Bradford zone.**

EXHIBIT 4a.
Version of the Bradford curve,
based on the data in Exhibit 3.

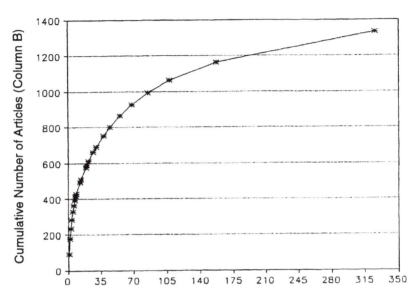

Cumulative Number of Journals (Column A)

Bradford law. *See* **Bradford's law.**

Bradford multiplicator. *See* **Bradford multiplier.**

Bradford multiplier. The n in the proportion $1{:}n{:}n^2{:}\ \ldots$ that is created when one groups sources and items into Bradford zones during a Bradford analysis. Also called **Bradford factor, Bradford multiplicator.**

For example, in the first *sample reference*, Bradford (1934) arranges lubrication journals from most to least productive and reports that:

      the top 8 journals produce 110 articles;
      the next 29 journals produce 133 articles;
      the next 127 journals produce 152 articles.

EXHIBIT 4b.
Version of the Bradford curve,
based on the data in Exhibit 3.

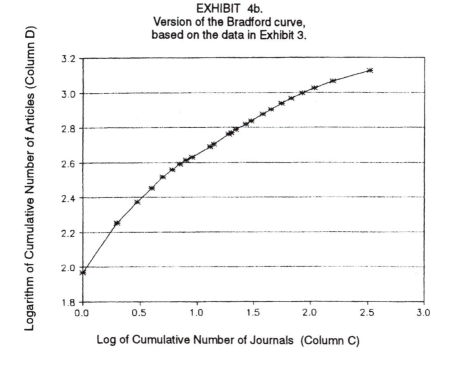

Log of Cumulative Number of Journals (Column C)

These three zones contain roughly the same number of articles. (That is a requirement for the creation of a zone.) The number of journals in the three zones are in this proportion: 8:29:127. A coarse approximation to this proportion is 1:4:17, which is approximately = $4^0:4^1:4^2$ or 1:4:16. Then, n = 4 in the general proportion given above ($1:n:n^2$ . . .). So, the Bradford multiplier in this example is about 4.

In the second *sample reference*, Egghe (1990b) examines the value of the multiplier in 16 Bradford analyses in various subject fields and compares the multiplier with the number of articles per journal.

Bradford nucleus. The first and most productive Bradford zone or group that results from doing a Bradford analysis. Also called **core, core zone, nuclear zone, nucleus.**

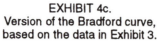

EXHIBIT 4c.
Version of the Bradford curve,
based on the data in Exhibit 3.

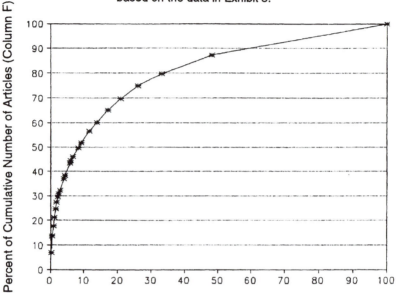

Percent of Cumulative Number of Journals (Column E)

The nucleus produces approximately the same number of items (usually articles) as do the other zones, but the nucleus contains only a few sources (usually journals). These are the most prolific sources (or core journals) in the collection being studied.

In the first *sample reference*, Bradford's own analysis (1934) of lubrication articles eight journals comprise the nucleus. They produce 28 percent of the articles from the entire collection of 154 journals.

In the second *sample reference*, Kirby (1991) analyzes 145 journals that produce 1,261 book reviews. The seven most productive journals comprise the nucleus and account for 34 percent (430) of the book reviews.

Bradford nucleus, minimum. A theoretical minimum for the number of items (usually articles) and sources (usually journals) in

EXHIBIT 4d.
Version of the Bradford curve,
based on the data in Exhibit 3.

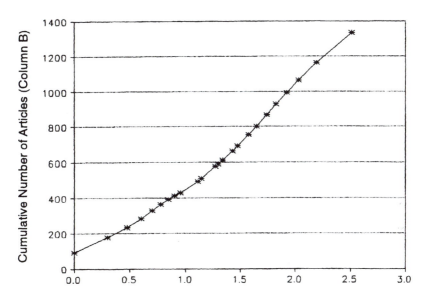

Log of Cumulative Number of Journals (Column C)

a Bradford nucleus. The smallest number of items in the nucleus is the smallest whole number greater than one-half the number of sources that contribute only one item each to the collection being analyzed. The smallest number of sources in the nucleus is one.

For example, if there are 135 journals that contribute one article each, then the nucleus has a theoretical minimum of $135/2 + 1/2 = 67.5 + 0.5 = 68$ articles. However, the actual minimum may be greater than 68 articles. Let us say that the three most productive journals contribute 50, 35, and 30 articles respectively. This means that the most productive journal generates fewer articles (50) than the theoretical minimum (68). Adding the second journal raises the actual minimum to $50 + 35 = 85$ articles, the sum of articles produced by the first two journals. In this example, the minimum size of the nucleus is 85 articles and two journals.

In the first *sample reference*, Goffman and Warren (1969) introduce this concept, calling it the "minimal nucleus" during an analysis of mast cell and schistomiasis literatures (p. 1206).

In the second *sample reference*, Brooks (1990) explains how this concept may be applied to deciding the Bradford multiplier and the Bradford partition of a collection of sources and items.

Bradford partition. The step in a Bradford analysis that divides sources and items into Bradford zones. How the partition is created and the nature of the subject field vary with values for the Bradford article cohort, Bradford multiplier(s), and the number of items and sources in the zones. Also called **partition**.

In the *sample reference*, Brooks (1990) creates Bradford partitions for eight collections of documents.

Bradford's law. One of the major laws of bibliometrics. It says that in a given subject field over a given period of time: (1) a few journals publish a relatively high percent of the articles in the field; (2) there are many journals that publish only a few articles each. Some bibliometricians use "sources" instead of "journals" and "documents" or "publications" or "items" instead of "papers" or "articles." Also called **Bradford distribution**; **Bradford law**; **Bradford's law of scattering**.

BASIC INFORMATION

The law is named for science librarian Samuel Clement Bradford (1878-1948). His original work is the first *sample reference*. Bradford (1934) examines bibliographies of applied geophysics (1928-1931) and lubrication (1931-33). He finds, for example, that in applied geophysics two of 326 journals are clearly the most prolific, producing 93 and 86 articles, respectively on the topic. Most (169) of the 326 journals produce one article each on applied geophysics.

Some readers think of this inverse relationship between number of articles and number of journals as the heart of Bradford's law. This idea is known as core and scatter. At one extreme are the most core journals, like the two prolific journals noted above in geophysics. At another extreme are the journals that produce only one article each on a topic. The articles here are said to be scattered among these journals. Therefore, Bradford's law is also known as Bradford's law of scattering and Bradford's law of dispersion.

In the second *sample reference,* Kirby (1991) identifies the most productive journals of book reviews on United States history. During a specified time, he finds that:

the top 7 journals produce 430 reviews;
the next 18 journals produce 419 reviews;
the next 120 journals produce 412 reviews.

The seven top ranked journals are the most productive journals in this analysis. They form the core of journals that contain book reviews in United States history. We also see that 412 of the reviews are scattered among 120 different journals.

In the third *sample reference,* Wallace (1987) describes the basics of Bradford's law and its applications to libraries.

ZONES AND PROPORTIONS

Bradford shows that the analyzed journals can be placed into groups that account for about the same number of articles each. The groups are called Bradford zones; the most prolific journals are in the zone called the Bradford nucleus or core. For example, after arranging the lubrication journals from most to least productive, Bradford (1934) finds that:

the top 8 journals produce 110 articles;
the next 29 journals produce 133 articles;
the next 127 journals produce 152 articles.

These three zones contain roughly the same number of articles. (That is a requirement for the creation of a zone.) The number of journals in the three zones are in this proportion: 8:29:127. This proportion is roughly equal to the proportion 1:4:17, which is

close to = $4^0{:}4^1{:}4^2$ or 1:4:16. Then, n = 4 in the general proportion
1:n:n². . . . The n is called the Bradford multiplier. Therefore, some
people think of Bradford's law as the proportion:

1:n:n²: . . . or $n^0{:}n^1{:}n^2$: . . . .

where:

n is the Bradford multiplier.

MODELS AND PROBABILITY DISTRIBUTIONS

Some people think of Bradford's law as one of the many mathematical functions or probability distributions that formalize Bradford's original work, which is more textual and graphical than
mathematical. It is possible to distinguish between: Bradford's law
(Bradford's textual and graphical description of the patterns he
reports); and the Bradford distribution (a mathematical function that
describes the patterns). Others view Bradford's law and the Bradford distribution as synonymous terms.

The fourth *sample reference*, Qiu (1990) analyzes 19 such Bradford distributions (sometimes called **models**) into categories such as
rank-cumulative, rank-noncumulative, and size-frequency. The
writer suggests that Bradford's own graphs correspond to the formula:

Y = A + B * log X

where:

Y is the portion of all articles found in the portion, X, of the most
   productive journals;

A and B are parameters that depend on the given situation;
log is the logarithm. (p. 655)

For example, Bradford (1934) reports that about 32 percent of
the papers in applied geophysics (429 of 1,332) were produced by
the top 3 percent (9 of 326) journals.

Determining these percentages for all of Bradford's applied

geophysics data would result in A = 0.950 and B = 0.170 (Qiu, 1990), or:

Y = 0.950 + 0.170 ∗ log X

The fifth *sample reference*, Brookes (1977), gives another general mathematical expression of Bradford's law:

G(r) = k ∗ ln [(a + r)/a]

where:

G(r) is the cumulative number of items produced;
r is the cumulative number of sources that produced the items;
a and k are parameters that depend on the given situation;
ln is the natural logarithm. (p. 205)

When one graphs the relationship between the number of articles in a subject field and the number of journals that produce them, the result is often a Bradford curve.

Bradford's law of scattering. *See* **Bradford's law**.

Bradford-Zipf curve. *See* **Bradford curve**.

Bradford zone. Also called **Bradford group, zone**. The zones are created during an analysis of Bradford's law. Each zone contains approximately the same number of items (usually articles). The upper zones are the most productive and contain relatively few sources (usually journals). The core or Bradford nucleus is the first and most productive zone.

In the first *sample reference*, Bradford (1934) groups 395 lubrication articles from 164 journals into three groups:

the 1st zone contains 8 journals that produce 110 articles;
the 2nd zone contains 29 journals that produce 133 articles;
the 3rd zone contains 127 journals that produce 152 articles.

In the second *sample reference*, Kirby (1991) analyzes 1,261 book reviews from 145 journals. He finds that:

the 1st zone contains 7 journals that produce 430 reviews;
the 2nd zone contains 18 journals that produce 419 reviews;
the 3rd zone contains 120 journals that produce 412 reviews.

In the third *sample reference*, Lancaster, Gondek, McCowan, and Reese (1991) compare the zone in which a journal falls with how accessible it is in a library. That is, is it shelved in the library? Is it stored nearby? Is it only available via interlibrary loan?

bridge paper. An article that helps people in an applied area of a subject field use information from the research area of their field. Compare with **popularization**. A bridge paper is meant for specialists and may appear in a trade journal; a popularization is meant for any layperson and may appear in a newspaper or popular magazine.

In the first *sample reference*, Lancaster, Diodato, and Li (1988) suggest that bridge papers may be especially appropriate to help engineers solve "practical engineering problems" and close "the gap between research and application." The writers list six characteristics of an ideal bridge paper (p. 297).

The second *sample reference* is itself a bridge paper about bibliometrics. Wallace (1987) describes bibliometric research in such a way that the readers can apply bibliometric tools in their day to day work in libraries.

Brookes' law. A bibliometric law that describes the number of items (such as articles) produced by a number of sources (such as journals). Brookes' law is named for information scientist B. C. Brookes (1910-1991). Compare with **Bradford's law, Leimkuhler's law**.

For a given subject field over a given period of time, collect many or all the items published. List the sources in rank order, with the most prolific first. Then, one version of Brookes' law is:

$$R(r) = a * \ln(br)$$

where:

$R(r)$ is the number of items produced cumulatively by the sources of ranks 1 through r;
a and b are parameters that depend on the field;
ln is the natural logarithm.

In the first *sample reference*, Egghe (1988b) provides an expression of Brookes' law similar to the one above (p. 54). Egghe compares Brookes' law with other bibliometric laws.

The second *sample reference* is one of Brookes' own papers (1969) on Bradford's law.

C

central citing publication. In an analysis of cocitation clusters, this is a document containing citations to documents that are all in the same cluster. The citing document need not be in that cluster.

In the *sample reference*, Braam, Moed, and van Raan (1991b) use central citing publications to enhance the differences among clusters.

Chall readability formula. *See* **Dale-Chall readability formula**.

channel, formal. *See* **communication, formal**.

channel, informal. *See* **communication, informal**.

Chernoff face. A computer generated diagram resembling a human face and capable of displaying data in many dimensions (from four to at least 18 dimensions). It is named for statistician Herman Chernoff (b. 1923).

The first *sample reference* is Chernoff's own introduction of the concept. He makes an interesting side comment:

> This approach is an amusing reversal of a common one in artificial intelligence. Instead of using machines to discriminate between human faces by reducing them to numbers, we discriminate between numbers by using the machine to do the brute labor of drawing faces and leaving the intelligence to the humans, who are still more flexible and clever. (1973, pp. 365-366)

In the second *sample reference*, Schubert and Braun (1992) use Chernoff face diagrams to display socioeconomic and scientometric data about developing countries. They say: "The present attempt is the first to apply *Chernoff's* quasi-4D representation of scientometric data" (p. 10).

citable document. Any document that has the potential of being cited by some other document. The concept is important in measures, like the impact factor, that measure this potential.

For example, the impact factor of specified issue(s) of a journal is the following ratio:

$$\frac{\text{the number of citations received by the articles in given issues of a journal}}{\text{the number of articles published in those issues}}$$

The articles are all citable documents, even if some (or all) do not get cited during the specified period.

citation. When document A is mentioned in document B, the mention is a citation. The mention may occur in the text of document B or in the endnotes, footnotes, bibliography, or reference list of document B.

For example, at the end of this entry there is mention of an article by Shepherd, Watters, and Cai. This mention is a citation from the dictionary to their article.

Sometimes the word "reference" is a synonym for "citation." However, to see how they can be distinguished, consider the example of document A being listed among the footnotes in document B. Then, one can say that:

    document B gives document A as a reference;
    document B refers to document A;
    document B cites document A;

    and that:

    document A receives a citation from document B;
    document A receives a reference from document B;
    document A is cited by document B.

Time provides a way to distinguish between the "reference" and "citation" terminology. All the references in this dictionary (including the sample reference by Shepherd, Watters, and Cai) were published before this dictionary was. The article by Shepherd, Watters, and Cai is cited by a document (namely this dictionary) that was published after their article was released.

Bibliometricians often bypass "reference" terminology and say that:

> document B cites document A;
> document A is cited by document B.

In the *sample reference*, Shepherd, Watters, and Cai (1990) provide a brief discussion of this terminological issue.

citation age. A measure of synchronous obsolescence (**obsolescence, synchronous**). The citation age between a document and one of the references that it cites is obtained by subtracting the publication date of the reference from the publication date of the citing document. When there is more than a single reference, one can calculate a mean citation age or median citation age.

citation analysis. A wide-ranging area of bibliometrics that studies the citations to and from documents. Such studies may focus on the documents themselves or on such matters as: their authors; the journals (if the documents are journal articles) in which the articles appear; the organizations or countries in which the documents are produced; the purpose of the citations.

Many entries in this dictionary deal with citation analysis. Most directly associated with it are those beginning:

> −citation . . .
> or
> −cocitation. . . .

In the first *sample reference*, Budd (1991) performs a citation analysis of documents that deal with academic libraries. Data include: journals with the most articles on this topic; format of materials cited (books, journals, proceedings, and so on); age of the cited materials; most frequently cited journals; most frequently cited individuals.

In the second *sample reference*, Delendick (1990) does a citation analysis of three journals in systematic botany. He reports such characteristics as: format (books versus articles) cited; age of the citations; the most highly cited journals.

In the third *sample reference*, Herubel (1991) describes how citation analyses of dissertations can be used to evaluate serials.

In the fourth *sample reference*, Schriek (1991) identifies and describes the 19 most highly cited United States Courts of Appeals cases since 1932.

citation behavior. How often, why, and how an author cites other authors, as well as whom the author cites. Compare with **citation, biased**; **citation rate**; **citation type**; **citation utility**; **citing, normative theory of**.

citation, biased. A citation that is inappropriate in some way. The bias may be an outright error, as when an author cites the wrong source of information. The bias may be the omission of a citation. Compare with **citation, internal**; **citation type**; **citing, normative theory of**; **uncitedness**.

The most definite case of bias is the citing of an author because that author is well known, even though a lesser known colleague is more deserving of the citation. Also called **Matthew effect**, **halo effect**.

In the *sample reference*, MacRoberts and MacRoberts (1989) discuss how these and other factors can confound a citation analysis.

citation categorization. *See* **citation type**.

citation consumption factor. *See* **consumption factor**.

citation count. *See* **citation rate**.

citation density. *See* **density, citation**.

citation factor. The number of citations received by a document or group of documents divided by the number of citations given by the document(s) during a certain time period. The citation factor is one of the elements of the **consumption factor** of a journal. Compare with **impact factor, influence weight**.

In the *sample reference*, Todorov and Glanzel (1988) include the citation factor in their descriptions of various journal citation measures.

citation frequency. *See* **citation rate.**

citation function. *See* **citation type.**

citation given and citation received. When document A mentions document B, then:

> document A gives a citation to document B, and
> document B receives a citation from document A.

This is equivalent to saying:

> document A cites document B, and
> document B is cited by document A.

citation index. An index in which the user may look up an author or a particular document and find out the authors and documents that have cited the given author or document.

Examples of citation indexes are the Institute for Scientific Information's: *Arts & Humanities Citation Index®*, *Science Citation Index®*, and *Social Sciences Citation Index®*.

In the *sample reference*, Shapiro (1992) notes that the development of bibliometrics owes some of its origins to tables of cited court cases published in the legal field during the past two and a half centuries.

citation, interjournal. A citation that occurs when an article in journal A cites an article in journal B. It is also known as a journal-to-journal citation. When these kind of data are recorded for a group of journals, the writer often displays them in a citation matrix, which some call a cross citation matrix.

In the *sample reference*, Everett and Pecotich (1991) analyze interjournal and intrajournal citations (**citation, intrajournal**) among marketing journals.

citation, internal. A mention of a work in the body of the citing document but not in the bibliography, endnotes, footnotes, or list of references of the citing document.

There are at least two types of internal citations. First, there are internal citations that provide little if any bibliographic data about the document mentioned. This occurs when a work is so well known in a field that the citing author feels that a brief mention of the work is sufficient. For example, a paper on bibliometrics may mention Bradford's law without ever formally citing any of Bradford's publications. Compare with **uncitedness**. Also called **noncitation**.

Second, there are internal citations that do contain complete bibliographic data within the body of the citing document but are not repeated in the references at the end of the citing document.

In the *sample reference*, Delendick (1990) calls the first case a noncitation, but some bibliometricians may wish to count such mentions as internal citations. In the *sample reference*, an example of the second case of internal citation occurs in systematic botany. Here lists of papers that name organisms may occur within the body of the paper but not necessarily in the list of references, unless the cited paper also appears in another context in the citing document.

citation, intrajournal. A citation in which a journal article cites another article from the same journal, though not necessarily from the same issue. One may consider an intrajournal citation to be a type of self citation.

In a citation matrix (or cross citation matrix), the intrajournal citation appears on the matrix diagonal. For example, in Exhibit 5 the diagonal entries from top left to bottom right are 2, 0, and 1. This means that journal A has two intrajournal citations; journal B has none; and journal C has one.

In the *sample reference*, Everett and Pecotich (1991) analyze intrajournal and interjournal citations (**citation, interjournal**) among marketing journals.

citation location. Where a citation is mentioned in a document. A bibliometrician may classify locations by labels found in the citing document (such as "Introduction," "Methodology," and "Conclusion") or by simply dividing the document into equal parts, such as thirds, quarters, or fifths.

In the *sample reference*, Cano (1989) studies the occurrence of citations in the beginning, middle, and end sections of documents.

citation matrix. A matrix that displays the citations among authors, documents, or journals. Also called **cross citation matrix**. It is commonly used to show citations among articles in various journals.

For example, Exhibit 5 is a matrix showing the number of citations among a small group of journals. This matrix indicates that journal A has cited journal A (itself) two times; journal A has cited journal B five times; journal C has cited journal A zero times; and so on.

A special type of citation matrix is the **cocitation matrix**, which usually indicates how often two authors or journals are simultaneously cited.

In the *sample reference*, Everett and Pecotich (1991) create a model based on an analysis of a citation matrix for 18 marketing journals.

citation motivation. *See* **citation type**.

citation network. The connections among a group of authors, documents, journals, or even a group of subject areas established by the citations among them. The network may be displayed graphically.

For example, the diagram in Exhibit 6 indicates that in a given field during a certain time period, author A has cited author B three times and has been cited four times by author B; authors C and B have cited each other two times; author D cites all the other authors, but is cited only by author E.

Unlike Exhibit 6, some pictures of citation networks are drawn so that the number of citations determines the thickness of the lines or the distances between the authors.

EXHIBIT 5.
A citation matrix.

		Citing Journals		
		A	B	C
Cited	A	2	2	0
Journals	B	5	0	6
	C	4	6	1

In the *sample reference*, Shepherd, Watters, and Cai (1990) discuss hypertext representations of citation networks.

citation, non-. *See* **citation, internal; uncitedness.**

citation, outside. A citation in which the citing document or the cited document is not in the group of documents being analyzed. However, the cited document is in the group.

In the first *sample reference*, Hicks and Potter (1991) analyze citations to a 313-item bibliography on the sociology of scientific knowledge. In their search of the *Social Sciences Citation Index®*, they find some citations to the bibliography that are from outside. That is, some of the citing documents are not in the bibliography and/or not by authors who publish in the field of the sociology of scientific knowledge.

In the second *sample reference*, Gatten (1991) determines the

EXHIBIT 6.
A citation network.

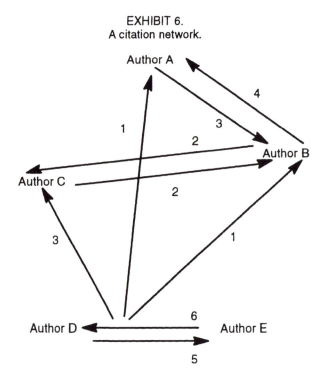

subject fields of the journals cited by articles in library science and in sociology. Some of the cited journals come from outside the respective fields of library science and sociology.

citation rate. Often refers to the number of citations an author, document, or journal has received during a certain period of time. Also called **citation count, citation frequency.**

If expressed as a ratio, especially for a group of documents published by a particular journal, citation rate becomes equivalent to impact factor. As a ratio, citation rate can be the number of citations received by the documents divided by the number of documents in the group.

citation received and citation given. When document A mentions document B, then:

> document A gives a citation to document B, and
> document B receives a citation from document A.

This is equivalent to saying:

> document A cites document B, and
> document B is cited by document A.

citation, self. See **autocitation; citation, intrajournal; self citation; self citation, hidden.**

citations, mutual. A situation in which two authors cite each other. Compare with **bibliographic coupling, cocitation.**

Assume that author A writes a paper in 1990 in which author B's 1988 article is one of the citations. A few years later in 1993, author B writes a paper in which a 1986 article by author A is cited. Therefore, authors A and B have received from each other (or given each other) mutual citations.

In Exhibit 6, arrows in both directions between A and B mean that there are mutual citations between A and B.

citation speed. *See* **mean response time; response time; time lag, citation.**

citation, successive. A citation to a publication that receives citations over successive years and even decades. This may occur, for example, when a publication is well known for many years as a seminal paper in its field.

The *sample reference* is one of many articles in which Vlachy (1983) tracks the citing of documents over the years. The resulting graphs display increases as well as decreases in the number of citations that documents receive.

citation taxonomy. *See* **citation type**.

citation threshold. *See* **cocitation threshold**.

citation time lag. *See* **time lag, citation**.

citation type. A classification of a citation by its purpose.

For example, the purpose of one citation may be to demonstrate the need for the research being reported; another citation may link its document with similar documents written by others.

Citation type also refers to the role that a citation plays in a document. Those who study citation behavior may be more interested in why an author includes a citation and how the reader uses it than in how many citations there are to or from a document. Also called **citation categorization**; **citation function**; **citation motivation**; **citation taxonomy**; **citer motivation**.

Compare with **citation, biased**; **citation utility**; **citing, normative theory of**.

In the first *sample reference*, Cano (1989) examines citation type (such as perfunctory and confirmative); utility level of the cited document to the citing document; and the location of the citation (**citation location**) in the document.

In the second *sample reference*, Warner (1991) classifies citations into types such as essential, supplementary, and review.

In the third *sample reference*, Frost (1979) classifies citations into types such as representing approval of the cited document, representing disapproval of the citing document, references to further reading, and acknowledgement of pioneering work.

citation, un-. *See* **uncitedness**.

citation utility. A measure of the importance of a citation to the citing author. Also called **utility level of citations**.

In the *sample reference*, Cano (1989) asks research subjects to rate the indispensability of citations to the production of their own papers.

cited document and citing document. If document A cites document B, then document A is the citing document and document B is the cited document.

Another way to say this is: document A mentions document B. The usual mention is a citation in document A's endnotes, footnotes, or list of references that gives bibliographic data for document B.

Similar definitions apply to cited and citing authors and journals.

cited half life. *See* **half life, cited**.

citer motivation. *See* **citation type**.

citing document and cited document. *See* **cited document and citing document**.

citing half life. *See* **half life, citing**.

citing, normative theory of. The assumption that an author cites another author for appropriate and useful reasons. If the assumption holds, then it is possible to analyze citations to make inferences about the value of the cited document and citing document and about the topics they discuss. This theory is related to the study of why authors cite and the various types (**citation type**) of citations they use or misuse (**citation, biased**).

In the first *sample reference*, Cronin (1981) notes that the norm under consideration is a norm of conduct in science:

> The successful working of the scientific system is dependent upon a voluntary and universal acceptance of these norms [of conduct in scientific enquiry] by the scientific establishment, and in this sense the citation convention relies more on consensual conviction than any explicit or enforceable code of conduct. (p. 21)

In the second *sample reference*, MacRoberts and MacRoberts (1987) evaluate the use of citations in the field of the history of genetics. In their introduction, they say: "The normative theory of citing holds that scientists 'reward' colleagues whose work they use by citing that work . . . [and] that authors should not cite preferentially. . . ." (p. 305).

cliometrics. The quantification of the study of history. At least some of cliometrics overlaps with bibliometrics, if it is assumed that the study of history involves the study of information. Compare with **econometrics**.

In the first *sample reference*, White and McCain (1989) say that "[b]ibliometrics is . . . [especially when using cocitation analysis] a form of cliometrics for those who study the social and intellectual history of a science. . . ." (p. 142).

In the second *sample reference*, Ritter (1986) notes there is confusion between cliometrics and terms like econometric history. However, "[C]liometrics logically implies any kind of (economic or otherwise) history that makes use of mathematical and statistical theory" (p. 121).

cluster. A collection of authors, documents, journals, or other entities that share some characteristics.

The cluster may be shown as a graph. For example, points representing members of the cluster may be close to each other on a graph or other diagram. The cocitation cluster map is such a diagram.

Evidence of the cluster may be shown quantitatively, using a cluster index. In the *sample reference*, Brooks (1990) notes that a low cluster index in a Bradford analysis indicates an unusually high proportion of singleton journals. Singleton journals contain only one article each on the given topic.

coauthorship. See **authorship, multiple**.

cocitation. The situation in which two (or more) authors, documents, or journals are simultaneously cited by another document. Compare with **bibliographic coupling; cocitation analysis, author; cocitation analysis, journal**.

For an example of cocitations, look at the approximately 200 items in the list of sample references at the end of this dictionary. These articles and books have all been cocited by the dictionary.

In Exhibit 7, assume that:

document I cites documents A, B, C, and D;
document II cites documents C, D, E, F and G.

Therefore:

many pairs of documents are cocited; for example, documents E and F are cocited (by document II); documents D and E are cocited (by document II); documents A and B are cocited (by document I); documents C and D are cocited (by document I and by document II);

also, documents I and II are bibliographically coupled because they both cite documents C and D; I and II would still be bibliographically coupled even if C were the only document that they both cited.

cocitation analysis, author. The study of cocitations between authors. It is analogous to journal cocitation analysis (**cocitation analysis, journal**), which deals with cocitations between journals.

For example, look at the bibliography at the end of an article in library and information science. If the bibliography lists articles by both Garfield and Lancaster, then these two authors are cocited by the bibliography. An author cocitation analysis may determine if there is a strong subject relationship between authors who are often cocited. If so, this suggests that subject searches could be done using pairs or groups of personal names.

The results of an author cocitation analysis may be displayed in a cocitation matrix.

The *sample reference* by Lunin and White (1990) is a special collection of articles on author cocitation analysis. The articles are written for the nonexpert in cocitation analysis.

EXHIBIT 7.
Cocited and bibliographically coupled documents.

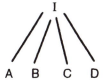

cocitation analysis, journal. The study of cocitations between journals. It is analogous to author cocitation analysis (**cocitation analysis, author**), which deals with cocitations between authors.

For example, look at the references in the bibliography at the end of an article in library and information science. If the bibliography lists articles from both the *Journal of Documentation* and *Scientometrics*, then those two journals have been cocited by the article. Journal cocitation analyses examine matters such as whether there is a tendency for *Scientometrics* to be cited whenever the *Journal of Documentation* is cited. Such an analysis may provide evidence that the cocited journals cover similar topics.

The results of a journal cocitation analysis may be displayed in a cocitation matrix.

In the first *sample reference*, McCain (1991c) performs a cocitation analysis of 35 economics journals.

In the second *sample reference*, McCain (1991b) demonstrates how cocitation analysis of 33 genetics journals may aid in managing a serials collection.

cocitation cluster map. A diagram that displays groups of authors, documents, or journals and the cocitations among them. The diagram groups the authors, documents, or journals so that cocitations tend to occur within groups rather than between them. Also called **cocitation map**.

Exhibit 8 is an example of a simple cocitation cluster map for three groups of authors. Clusters A, B, and C respectively contain five, seven, and three authors. A point represents each author. The closer two points are to each other, the more they tend to be cocited. An author in one cluster is far away from authors in all other clusters, but there may still be some cociting between authors in different clusters. The relative distances between the clusters shows how much of this intercluster cociting exists.

In Exhibit 8, look at cluster B. Authors 8 and 9 are so close together that they must get cocited more than any other pair in the diagram. Authors 8 and 10 get cocited much less often. Cociting within cluster B is much more frequent than cociting between authors in B and authors in clusters C or A.

The distance between points and clusters and sometimes even the thickness of lines joining points or clusters are based on such measures as citation frequency, cocitation strength, cocitation threshold, and distance between cocited documents. A cluster or group of clusters may represent a subject specialty, school of thought, or research front.

In the first *sample reference*, Braam, Moed, and van Raan (1991b) create a 20-cluster cocitation cluster map of research in a specialty of atomic and molecular physics. The clusters are arranged chronologically from top to bottom in the map.

In the second *sample reference*, McCain (1990) creates a 10-cluster cocitation cluster map of research in macroeconomics. The clusters are arranged on a two-dimensional grid to show distances within and between the clusters.

EXHIBIT 8.
A cocitation cluster map for groups of authors.

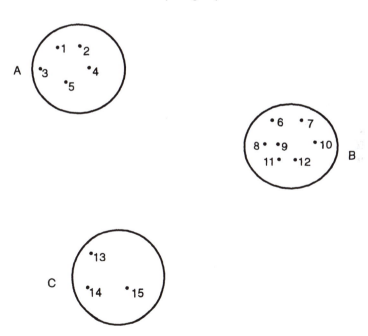

cocitation map. See **cocitation cluster map**.

cocitation matrix. A type of citation matrix that shows authors, documents, or journals that are cocited.

An example of an author cocitation matrix is in Exhibit 9. It indicates that in an analysis of documents, there are 15 documents that each cite both Bowa and Aron. There are no documents that cocite Dath and Cort. There are 11 documents that cocite Bowa and Cort.

In the *sample reference*, McCain (1990) provides an overview of the techniques used in cocitation matrixes.

cocitation strength. A measure of the cocitation link between two authors, documents, or journals by comparing their cocitations to all the citations they receive. Ideally, the measure of cocitation strength should be equal to one in the unlikely situation of two items receiving only cocitations and never being cited individually.

In the *sample reference*, Garfield (1986a) suggests the following ratio for the cocitation strength between documents A and B:

$$\frac{\text{number of cocitations of A and B}}{(\text{number of citations of A}) + (\text{number of citations B}) - (\text{number of cocitations of A and B})}$$

For example, if document A receives 50 citations, of which ten are cocitations with document B, and if document B receives 160 citations (of which ten have to be cocitations with document A), then the cocitation strength between A and B is:

$$\frac{10}{50 + 160 - 10} = 0.05$$

cocitation threshold. The minimum values of certain parameters that allow authors, documents, or journals to be included in a cluster of a cocitation cluster map. The parameters are the frequency of citations received by each document and the cocitation strength between pairs of documents. Sometimes, the cocitation threshold refers only to the minimum value of the cocitation strength. Also called **citation threshold, threshold**.

EXHIBIT 9.
A cocitation matrix for authors.

	Bowa	Cort	Dath
Aron	15	28	7
Bowa		11	13
Cort			0

In the *sample reference*, Garfield (1986a) notes that selecting documents with at least 20 citations and a citation strength of at least 0.24 will result in a smaller cluster than if the threshold values are 17 citations and 0.22 citation strength.

cohort. *See* **Bradford article cohort**.

Cole slope. *See* **slope, Cole**.

collaboration. May be used synonymously with multiple authorship (**authorship, multiple**) or coauthorship. However, collaboration also refers to the broader concept of two or more researchers (or researchers from two or more organizations or countries) working together.

communication, boundary-spanning. Communication of members of one group with members of another group. This concept is important in the study of scholarly communication. Compare with **science-profession dyad**.

In the *sample reference*, Weedman (1992) examines formal and informal communication (**communication, formal**; **communication, informal**) among members of three groups: editors, reviewers, and scholar/critics.

communication, formal. Communication, usually between scholars, scientists, or other professionals, that is recorded and indexed for later retrieval. Also called formal channel (**channel, formal**).

Examples include a book, a journal article, and a speech that appears in the proceedings of a conference. Some writers may call each of these examples a formal channel through which the communication flows.

In the *sample reference*, Lancaster (1978) contrasts formal communication as being less interactive and less oral than informal communication (**communication, informal**) (p. 52).

communication, informal. Communication, usually between scholars, scientists, or other professionals, that does not appear in published form. Also called informal channel (**channel, informal**).

Examples include a speech at a conference that does not appear in a proceedings, a telephone conversation, and a committee discussion. Some writers may call each of these examples an informal channel through which the communication flows.

In the *sample reference*, Lancaster (1978) contrasts informal communication as being more interactive and more oral than formal communication (**communication, formal**) (p. 52).

complete count. One way to determine how many documents a person has authored. This is an issue when one is analyzing publications with multiple authors (**authorship, multiple**). Also called **normal count**. Compare with **adjusted count, straight count**.

For an example of the complete count, assume there are four documents with the following authors:

Document 1 is authored by Queen, Jack, and King;
Document 2 is authored by Jack;
Document 3 is authored by King and Queen.
Document 4 is authored by Jack and Jill.

When doing a complete count, the rule is to count every author fully whenever he/she appears, whether or not there is multiple authorship. Therefore, in the above list, Queen has two publications (documents 1 and 3); Jack has three publications (documents 1, 2, and 4); King has two publications (documents 1 and 3); and Jill has one publication (document 4).

How to count authors is important when working with Lotka's law and sometimes in doing a citation analysis.

In the first *sample reference*, Lindsey (1980) describes advantages and disadvantages of various ways to count authors.

In the second *sample reference*, Nicholls (1989) examines 30 studies of Lotka's law and indicates how each researcher counts authorship.

concentration. The high productivity displayed by a relatively few sources. Also called **inequality**.

Some laws of bibliometrics say that many of the articles in a subject field are produced by a relatively few sources (like the prolific authors in Lotka's law and the core journals in Bradford's law). The articles are concentrated in these prolific authors and core journals.

Some may see concentration as: (1) synonymous with, and/or (2) occurring simultaneously with diversity or dispersion. Bibliometric laws can demonstrate concentration and diversity at the same time. For example, in Lotka's law, diversity means that some documents in a subject field are scattered among many nonprolific authors, who produce only one or two documents each.

In the *sample reference*, Egghe and Rousseau (1991) analyze various measures of concentration.

consumption factor. A way to measure the impact of a journal. The consumption factor is a combination of two other characteristics of journal citations: the citation factor and the popularity factor. Also called **citation consumption factor, journal consumption factor**. Compare with **impact factor**.

The consumption factor of journal A during a certain time period is its citation factor multiplied by its popularity factor:

$$\text{citation factor * popularity factor}$$

or

$$\frac{\text{number of citations received by the articles in journal A}}{\text{number of citations in the articles in journal A}} * \frac{\text{number of journals that cite the articles in journal A}}{\text{number of journals that are cited by the articles in journal A}}$$

For example, examine journal A and a group of other journals in the same subject field for the period 1994-95. Assume the following information about these journals has been collected:

articles in journal A contain 460 citations during 1994-95; these
citations are to 45 different journals;
articles in journal A are cited 125 times during 1994-95;
these citations are from 15 different journals.

Then, the consumption factor of journal A is:

$$\frac{125}{460} * \frac{15}{45} = 0.27 * 0.33 = 0.09$$

In the first *sample reference* Yanovsky (1981) introduces the
consumption factor and shows how to calculate it for scientific
journals.

In the second *sample reference*, Todorov and Glanzel (1988)
include the consumption factor as one of several journal citation
measures that they discuss.

content analysis. An analysis of the textual and nontextual elements of a document.

A textual analysis may examine the numbers, types and positions
of characters, words, phrases, sentences, paragraphs, and sections.
Textual analysis may also examine the readability index of a document.

A nontextual analysis may examine the numbers, types and positions of charts, figures, graphs, tables, and other illustrations.

In the first *sample reference*, Snizek, Oehler, and Mullins (1991)
study relationships between the number of citations a document
receives and various elements of the document, such as the number
of figures and pages.

In the second *sample reference*, Tibbo (1992) does a content
analysis of 120 abstracts in chemistry, history, and psychology. He
reports such data as words per abstract, words per sentence, and the
percent of sentences in the abstracts devoted to categories such as
hypotheses, methodology, purpose/scope, and results.

In the third *sample reference*, Reser and Schuneman (1992) use
content analysis to compare library public service and library technical service job advertisements.

content word. In the first sense, this is a word that names something (a noun); indicates an action (a verb); or describes something (adjective or adverb). This is contrasted with a function word such as a preposition or article. In analysis of text, some researchers examine only the content words. In the title, "All Cats Go to Heaven," all words but "to" may be considered content words.

In the second sense, this is a word that conveys at least part of the meaning of a document. Being a content word in the first sense above is necessary but may not be sufficient to being a content word in the second sense. In the above title, "All" is a word with content in the first sense, but by itself it tells very little about the content of the document. If the word "loyalty" appears in the document and conveys some of the meaning of the document, it is a content word in the second sense, even if it is not a title word.

In the *sample reference*, Braam, Moed, and van Raan (1991a) note that titles are limited sources of content words.

core. *See* **Bradford nucleus; core and scatter; core journal; core zone**.

core and scatter. The idea that a comprehensive search of a given topic over a given period of time will uncover a collection of items (usually articles) from various sources (usually journals) with the following two characteristics.

First, a few of the journals will be very productive and account for many more articles than any of the other journals. These few comprise the core.

Second, many journals will be very unproductive and publish only one or two articles each on the given topic during the specified time period. Articles in these journals are said to be scattered among the journals.

The core and scatter idea is based on findings from studies of Bradford's law. Also called **Bradford's law of scattering, core**.

core journal. A journal that produces many of the articles on a particular topic. One or more core journals appear during a comprehensive search of a given topic over a specified time period. Bradford's law predicts that there will be relatively few core journals for a given topic. The core journals are found in the Bradford nucleus, also called **core**.

For example, assume that a comprehensive search for articles on a certain topic over a given period of time identifies 1,520 articles in 200 journals. After ranking them, from most productive journals to least (in this subject area), they divide into the following groups or Bradford zones:

> 1st zone: 10 journals that produce 505 articles;
> 2nd zone: 22 journals that produce 495 articles;
> 3rd zone: 168 journals that produce 520 articles.

The first zone contains the core journals. These ten produce, in this example, about 1/3 of the 1,520 articles found on this topic.

core zone. The most productive Bradford zone or group that results from doing a Bradford analysis. Also called **Bradford nucleus**, **core**. In the core are the relatively few sources, often journals, that produce relatively large numbers of publications, often articles. Therefore, it is said that the core zone contains the core journals.

In the *sample reference*, Brooks (1990) notes that it has been difficult to determine reliable sizes of core zones.

count. *See* **adjusted count**; **complete count**; **publication count**; **straight count**.

coverage. The journals indexed by an indexing service. One may express coverage by listing the names of the journals, counting them, or specifying their subject areas. Coverage is most important in bibliometrics in analyses of coverage overlap. Also called **index coverage**, **journal coverage**.

coverage overlap. The journals that are indexed simultaneously by two indexing services. Also called **overlap**.

The overlap may be expressed as the number of journals common to the services. One also may express overlap using a ratio of intersection and union, like the following:

$$\frac{\text{number of journals in (A intersection B)}}{\text{number of journals in (A union B)}}$$

where:

A is the list of journals indexed by one indexing service;

B is the list of journals indexed by another indexing service;

A intersection B is the list of only those journals simultaneously indexed by the two indexing services;

A union B is the list of all the journals indexed by one or the other or both indexing services.

For example, assume that the Ace Index indexes 55 journals and the Bright Index indexes 135 journals. Also assume that 25 journals are common to the two services. We know immediately that 25 is the size of their intersection. In describing the size of their union, it is important to count unique journals and to omit duplicates; the size of their union is $55 + 135 - 25 = 165$. Therefore, the above ratio becomes:

$$\frac{25}{55 + 135 - 25} = \frac{25}{165} = 0.15$$

In comparing indexes that are online or compact disc databases, one may get data for the overlap study by doing an identical search in each database. (There are also studies of online and compact disc databases that use overlap to refer to the documents that are simultaneously retrieved from two databases using the same search. This kind of analysis is closer to information retrieval analysis than bibliometric analysis.)

In the first *sample reference*, Burnham, Shearer, and Wall (1992) search for information on the topic of gait in MEDLINE and CINAHL compact disc databases. They find articles from 25 different journals:

5 of the journals are exclusively in CINAHL;

18 of the journals are exclusively in MEDLINE

2 of the journals are in both databases.

Therefore, the coverage overlap for CINAHL and MEDLINE for this search would be: $2/25 = 0.04$.

In the second *sample reference*, Snow (1984) calculates overlap in the coverage of 337 pharmaceutical journals by seven online indexing services. Therefore, there are six overlap scores for each of the seven services.

In the third *sample reference*, Gluck (1990) suggests an extension to the definition of overlap.

coword analysis. An analysis of the cooccurrence of two or more words in one document or in different documents. The words may be (1) keywords or (2) text words.

KEYWORDS AS COWORDS

The analysis of co-occurring keywords usually means examining the indexing terms assigned to documents by an indexing service or by the authors of the documents. For example, if a group of documents all have "networks" and "technology" as two of their indexing terms, those two terms are said to co-occur in that group of documents. This may be evidence that the papers in the group have a common subject. As in the analysis of cocitations, the analysis of cowords indicates how similar documents are and identifies clusters of documents on the same topic. The basis for the data collection may be development of a word profile for each of the documents. As in a cocitation cluster map, a coword analysis may be displayed as a map of clusters of documents.

In the first *sample reference*, King (1987) describes coword analysis as an alternative to cocitation analyses. Cocitation analysis can become dependent on tools like *Science Citation Index®*, which have English-language and subject emphases.

In the second *sample reference*, Law and Whittaker (1992) examine the co-occurrence of index terms in documents on acidification. The co-ocurrence of the indexing terms allows the writers to identify groups or clusters of documents. Each cluster seems to deal with a particular theme within the field of acidification research.

TEXTWORDS AS COWORDS

The analysis of cooccurring text words is another way to identify commonalities among documents. Such research overlaps with research in the field of information retrieval.

In the third *sample reference*, Leydesdorff (1991) applies the textword technique to the field of scientometrics. For example, cooccurrence of a word and its synonym in the same sentence of a scientific paper suggests special importance for that sentence. This kind of analysis throughout all the sentences of the paper may allow a reconstruction of the development of the ideas that went into creation of the paper.

cross citation matrix. *See* **citation matrix.**

cumulative advantage. The idea that bibliometric laws like Bradford's law and Lotka's law rely on the success breeds success phenomenon.

For example, a best selling author becomes even more of a best seller (and hence more dominant over other authors) as more and more readers become aware of the author's work. Compare with **Matthew effect.**

In the first *sample reference*, Price (1976) indicates that a highly cited paper is more likely to be cited again than is an infrequently cited paper.

In the second *sample reference*, Bensman (1985) suggests that cumulative advantage occurs in libraries when the chances that a book will be used in the future increase if it has been used in the past.

cumulative distribution function. *See* **distribution; model.**

currency. A measure of the up-to-dateness of a document. The document in question is often a journal article or an index to journal articles.

For example, one may examine the time that elapses between the submission of a manuscript and the publication of it; or the time that elapses between publication of an article and its being indexed. One may compare the currency of various formats of an index (compact disc, online, paper), or the currency of competing indexes.

Compare with **half life; immediacy index; mean citation age; median citation age; Price's index; recency score; time lag, citation; time lag, indexing;** and **time lag, publishing.**

In the first *sample reference*, Budd (1988) calculates for various library and information science journals the time between submission of a manuscript and its acceptance or rejection by the editor and then the time it takes to publish an accepted article.

In the second *sample reference*, McKinin, Sievert, and Collins (1991) compare three online indexes. For each of 64 journals, they determine the most recent date of the articles indexed by CCML and MEDLINE. Similarly, they compare the recency of the MEDIS and MEDLINE online indexes.

D

Dale-Chall readability formula. A readability index that describes the grade level appropriate for reading a given text. An examination of readability can be one step in doing a content analysis. Also called **Chall readability formula**. Compare with **Danielson and Bryan readability index, Flesch readability ease score, FOG readability index**.

The Dale-Chall formula is named for educators Edgar Dale (b. 1900) and Jeanne Sternlicht Chall (b. 1921).

In the first *sample reference*, Chall (1958) gives the formula as:

$$C_{50} = .1579X_1 + .0496X_2 + 3.6365$$

where:

C_{50} is the reading grade;
X_1 is the percent of words in the text that are not found in a vocabulary list called the "Dale 3,000";
X_2 is the average (mean) words per sentence in the text (p. 52).

In the second *sample reference*, Chall and Conrad (1991) note that a new version of the formula is in preparation (p. 41).

Danielson and Bryan readability index. A formula that counts the number of characters, words, and titles in a collection of documents. It was created as a readability index for computer science. It has also served as an index of complexity of the content of a title (**title analysis**). Compare with **Dale-Chall readability formula, Flesch readability ease score, FOG readability index**.

In the *sample reference*, White and Hernandez (1991) use the index to test whether titles of articles become more complex as a field matures. The formula is:

131.059 −
    [10.364 * (number of characters)/(number of words)] −
    [0.194 * (number of characters)/(number of titles)],

where the data refer to the number of characters, words, and titles in the group of titles being tested.

decay. *See* **obsolescence.**

density, citation. The fraction of a group of citable documents that are indeed cited. Citation density is sometimes used in studies of obsolescence. Also called **reference density, density of use.** Compare with **impact factor.**

Do not confuse citation density with the density ratio of references in a document to the size of the document.

For an example of citation density, look at all the citations (**references**) at the ends of the articles in the 1993 issues of Journal A. Find out how many of these citations refer to articles in the 1980 issues of Journal A. Assume that of 550 citations listed in 1993, only 25 are to the 1980 edition of Journal A. We also determine that in 1980, Journal A published 275 articles. Then, the citation density for citations from the 1993 Journal A to the 1980 Journal A is $25/275 = 0.09$.

In the first *sample reference*, Gupta (1990) measures the annual citation density of a physics journal, during an obsolescence study of the journal.

In the second *sample reference*, Heisey (1988) measures citation density (which the writer calls reference density) in a study of diasynchronous obsolescence (**obsolescence, diasynchronous**) of the Dead Sea Scrolls literature. This analysis goes beyond a single journal and covers an entire subject area.

density of use. *See* **density, citation.**

density ratio. A ratio of the number of references in a document's bibliography to the size of the document.

Also called **reference density,** but do not confuse with citation density (**density, citation**).

In the *sample reference*, Kidd (1990) uses the density ratio to calculate a hot topic index for a document. In this case, the density ratio is the number of references in a document per 1,000 words in the text of the document.

descriptive bibliometrics. *See* **bibliometrics, descriptive.**

diachronous obsolescence. *See* **obsolescence, diachronous**.

diasynchronous obsolescence. *See* **obsolescence, diasynchronous**.

disciplinary structure. In a subject field, the characteristics that determine how scholars in the field interact with each other and with the field as a whole. Structure consists of such factors as: who cites whom; what areas of research are pursued by new members of the discipline; the spread of new ideas; and how members of the discipline compete for research funds.

In the *sample reference*, Bricker (1991) uses author cocitation analysis to test the hypothesis that disciplinary structure may be hierarchical. At the top of the hierarchy is research utility, which is affected by the rewards and costs of the research, each of which, in turn, is affected by other factors.

discometrics. A type of bibliometrics that gathers data from discographies–lists of musical recordings, scores, and related documents.

In the *sample reference*, Rorick (1987) coins the term and describes its application to the development of a music collection. As an example, a discometric analysis displays the number of recordings of each of the nine symphonies of Ludwig van Beethoven. (Symphony number five has the most recordings; symphony number two has the least).

dispersion. According to many laws of bibliometrics, some of the items being analyzed (such as articles in a subject field) are spread or scattered among many different sources (such as authors in Lotka's law and journals in Bradford's law). Also called **diversity**. Compare with **concentration; inequality**.

In the *sample reference*, Rousseau (1992) proposes a model to describe measures of dispersion/diversity and concentration.

distance between cocited documents. The inverse of the cocitation strength between the documents. Therefore, two documents that have a high cocitation strength will have a smaller distance between them than two documents with a low cocitation strength. On a cocitation cluster map this measure indicates the relative positions of the points for the documents.

distance between journals. A measure of how dissimilar two journals are, based on their citations to each other or citations to other journals. The more unalike two journals are, the greater the distance between them.

For example, assume that the citation matrix in Exhibit 10a gives the number of citations among three journals.

Speaking imprecisely, Exhibit 10a suggests that journals A and B are similar to each other in the sense that they both cite each of the three journals about the same number of times. They both cite journal A two times. They cite journal B either five or six times. They cite journal C either one or two times. On the other hand, journals B and C seem to be dissimilar; for example, journal B cites journal A two times, while journal C cites journal A six times. So, in this example the distance between journals A and B should be smaller than the distance between journals B and C.

An example of how to precisely measure distance between journals requires transforming the citation matrix in Exhibit 10a into a new matrix that shows what portion of all a journal's citations go to each of the other journals. The new matrix is in Exhibit 10b. The entries in Exhibit 10b mean, for example, that 5/8 (five of eight) of journal A's citations are to journal B.

The following calculation of distance uses the three fractions in each journal's column in the transformed matrix.

$$\text{distance between A and B} = (2/8 - 2/10)^2 \\ + (5/8 - 6/10)^2 \\ + (1/8 - 2/10)^2 \\ = 0.009$$

and

$$\text{distance between B and C} = (2/10 - 6/12)^2 \\ + (6/10 - 0/12)^2 \\ + (2/10 - 6/12)^2 \\ = 0.54$$

By this method, the distance between A and B is much smaller than the distance between B and C. There are many other ways one could calculate the distance or dissimilarity between journals. Compare with **similarity**.

EXHIBIT 10a.
A citation matrix.

		Citing Journals		
		<u>A</u>	<u>B</u>	<u>C</u>
	<u>A</u>	2	2	6
Cited				
	<u>B</u>	5	6	0
Journals				
	<u>C</u>	1	2	6

EXHIBIT 10b.
A transformation of the citation matrix of Exhibit 10a, based on the number of citations in each column.

		Citing Journals		
		<u>A</u>	<u>B</u>	<u>C</u>
	<u>A</u>	2/8	2/10	6/12
Cited				
	<u>B</u>	5/8	6/10	0/12
Journals				
	<u>C</u>	1/8	2/10	6/12

In the *sample reference*, Robinson (1991) employs a measure like the one shown here to compare journals in economics.

distribution. Usually a mathematical expression that is also called a probability distribution function. Among the many employed in bibliometrics are the negative binomial distribution, Poisson distribution, and the Waring distribution.

The bibliometric laws can be expressed in terms of distributions.

Therefore, some writers say that these laws are distributions. This means there is a distinction between the verbal expression of a bibliometric law and the expression of the law as a distribution. Most of this dictionary's entries for bibliometric laws do not express this distinction and simply talk about the laws as laws.

An example of the distinction is seen in Bradford's law. Some say the law follows from the fact that in a given subject field, journals can be ranked into increasingly larger groups. All the groups produce about the same number of articles. The smallest group represents the core journals. The largest group is where one finds articles scattered, often at the rate of one article per journal. This idea does not get any more mathematical other than to say that the number of journals in the various groups often satisfy a certain ratio.

When Bradford's law is expressed as a distribution, the ideas of core and scatter are formalized into a mathematical expression. The *sample reference* (Brookes, 1977) gives an example of such a distribution:

$$G(r) = k * \ln [(a + r)/a]$$

where:

G(r) is the cumulative number of items (journal articles, for example) produced;
r is the cumulative number of sources (journals, for example) that produced the items;
a and k are parameters that depend on the given situation;
ln is the natural logarithm.

Distribution is also used loosely to be synonymous with terms like: **cumulative distribution function, frequency distribution, frequency distribution function, mathematical function, model,** and **probability distribution.**

diversity. Sometimes used synonymously with dispersion. Other times it has a specialized meaning. Compare with **concentration, inequality.**

When used synonymously with dispersion, diversity describes the common finding that in a subject field many of the articles are produced by many different authors (**Lotka's law**) and many different journals (**Bradford's law**).

In its specialized meaning, diversity refers to laws for the physical scatter of organisms in geographic areas. Such laws of diversity include the Margalef diversity index and Willis' law. In the *sample reference*, Magurran (1988) reviews and gives examples of how to calculate diversity measures in ecology.

document. Any kind of recorded information. The word is often used synonymously with publication. However, document is a broader word because documents include one of a kind items like personal diaries and the only copy of a student's term paper. Documents do not have to be in paper or print form.

dyad. See **science-profession dyad**.

E

e. The number that is equal to 2.71828. . . . It is the number whose natural logarithm is equal to 1. It is used in various calculations, such as in figuring the growth rate of a literature or the mean response time of a journal.

echo factor. A measure of the citations received by a journal. It is similar to but not identical with the journal impact factor.

In the *sample reference*, Zmaic, Maricic and Simeon (1989) develop the measure and define it as follows:

$$N_e = \frac{(N_{ind,a})_p}{(C_p S_a)}$$

where:

N_e is the echo factor for a journal;
$(N_{ind,a})_p$ is the number of independent citations received in year p by the articles that had been published in year a by the journal;
C_p is the number of potentially citing articles in year p;
S_a is the number of articles published by the journal in year a.
   (p. 175)

For example, assume that a certain journal publishes 50 articles in 1990. In 1993, 22 of these 50 articles are cited by articles in 15 journals. During 1993 these 15 journals publish a total of 340 articles. Therefore, in this example:

$(N_{ind,a})_p = (N_{ind,1990})_{1993} = 22;$
$C_p = 340;$
$S_a = 50.$

So, the echo factor for this journal is:

$$N_e = \frac{22}{(340 * 50)} = 0.00129$$

econometrics. A quantification of the study of economics. Econometrics overlaps with bibliometrics when they share principles that are conceptually or mathematically similar.

The concept of inequality is a place where econometrics and bibliometrics overlap. Econometricians develop mathematical expressions to analyze the uneven distribution of wealth. Bibliometricians see that this idea is also pervasive in bibliometric laws. For example, Lotka's law suggests that some authors are more prolific (wealthier) than most other authors in a given field.

In the first *sample reference*, Atkinson (1970) (an economist) develops formulas to measure imbalance of wealth and economic inequalities.

In the second *sample reference*, Egghe and Rousseau (1991) (informetricians) see some of Atkinson's mathematical expressions as sharing characteristics with other laws of bibliometrics (p. 481).

According to the third *sample reference*,

> Econometrics is a rapidly developing branch of economics which, broadly speaking, aims to give empirical content to economic relations. . . . By emphasizing the quantitative aspects of economic problems, econometrics calls for a "unification" of measurement and theory in economics. (Pesaran, 1987, p. 8)

80/20 rule. *See* **Trueswell's 80/20 rule**.

endogenous document. A document that reports on research that the author(s) conduct in the organization or country with which they are usually associated. Compare with **exogenous document**.

In the *sample reference*, Meneghini (1992) analyzes endogenous and exogenous document production in Brazilian biochemistry.

Erdos number. A somewhat whimsical though intriguing measure that could be applied beyond its narrow definition. The Erdos number of a mathematician equals one if the mathematician has coauthored a paper with mathematician Paul Erdos (b. 1913). It equals two if the mathematician has not coauthored a paper with Erdos but has coauthored a paper with someone else who has coauthored a paper with Erdos; and so on.

In the *sample reference*, the biographer (Tierney, 1984) notes that Erdos is a prolific author of over 1,000 papers and has had over 250 different coauthors.

Estroup's law. Identical to Zipf's first law (**Zipf's law**).

In the *sample reference*, Booth (1967) says the law was "first stated by [J. B.] Estroup (1916) and popularized by Zipf. . . ." The law initially appeared in a 1916 work called *Gammes stenographiques* (pp. 386, 392).

Euler's constant or **Euler's number.** The number 0.5772 . . . It is named for mathematician Leonhard Euler (1707-1783). Euler's number is the limit of the series:

$F(x) = 1 + 1/2 + 1/3 + . . . + 1/n - \ln n,$

where:

$F(x)$ is the value of the above formula for a given value of n, as n increases from 1 to 2 to 3, and so on;
ln is the natural logarithm.

The value of $F(x)$ becomes closer and closer to Euler's constant as n becomes greater.

In the *sample reference*, Rousseau (1990b) notes that Euler's constant is sometimes used in expressions of some versions of Zipf's law.

exogenous document. A document that reports on research that the author(s) conduct outside of the organization or country with which they are usually associated. Compare with **endogenous document**, **attraction power of a journal**.

In the *sample reference*, Meneghini (1992) analyzes endogenous and exogenous document production in Brazilian biochemistry.

expected citation rate. *See* **impact factor, expected**.

expected impact factor. *See* **impact factor, expected**.

exponential growth. *See* **growth rate**.

F

first author. *See* **author, primary.**

Flesch index. *See* **Flesch readability ease score.**

Flesch readability ease score. One of many formulas used to calculate the readability index of a document. An examination of readability can be one step in doing a content analysis. Also called **Flesch index.** Compare with **Dale-Chall readability formula, Danielson and Bryan readability index, FOG readability index.**

The Flesch readability ease score is named for rhetorician Rudolph F. Flesch (b. 1911).

In the first *sample reference*, Flesch (1974) describes the measure:

> Multiply the average sentence length [in number of words] by 1.015
> Multiply the number of syllables per 100 words by .846
> Add [the results from the first two steps]
> Subtract this sum from 206.835. (p. 250)

In the second *sample reference*, Shaw (1989) uses a software package that calculates the Flesch score and three other readability measures for an analysis of online search user manuals.

FOG readability index. A readability index based on the length of sentences and complexity of words in a text. It is expressed as a grade level. An examination of readability can be one step in doing a content analysis. Compare with **Dale-Chall readability formula, Danielson and Bryan readability index, Flesch readability ease score.**

In the first *sample reference*, the writer and developer of FOG (Gunning, 1968) describes how to calculate the readability of a text:

> Jot down the number of words in successive sentences. If the piece is too long, you may wish to take several samples of 100

words, spaced evenly through it. . . . Divide the total number of words in the passage by the number of sentences. . . .

Count the number of words of three syllables or more per 100 words. [Omit proper names, combined words like "book-keeper," and three syllable verbs made by adding -es or -ed, as "created."]

To get the Fog Index, total the two factors just counted and multiply by .4 (p. 38).

The name of the FOG Index comes from: (1) fogginess being the opposite of clarity; and (2) according to the second *sample reference*, the acronym for Frequency of Gobbledegook (Harrison, 1980, p. 79).

In the third *sample reference*, Meadows (1991) uses the FOG index to measure the readability of science reports in newspapers.

formal communication. *See* **communication, formal.**

frequency distribution. *See* **distribution; model.**

frequency distribution function. *See* **distribution; model.**

function. *See* **model.**

function, mathematical. *See* **distribution; model.**

G

gatekeeper. An individual who provides information to one group of people from another group. The gatekeeper often voluntarily takes on this activity as a member of the first (or inside) group.

The inside group is usually a well defined group, such as all the members of a certain department in an organization. The source of the information (or the outside group) may be well defined (such as all the members in another department in the organization) or may be ill defined (such as everybody in the world whom the gatekeeper will meet in the next 20 years and who is not in the gatekeeper's inside group).

For example, a gatekeeper may be an individual who is sent from home to study a specialty in another country for which there is no degree program at home. The gatekeeper eventually receives an academic degree, but more importantly returns home and shares the information learned with others in the originating country.

A less formal example is the individual who knows about the special interests of all others in a department and regularly stuffs colleagues' mail boxes with photocopies and electronic mail messages about new publications and products that the gatekeeper has heard of.

In the first *sample reference*, Lewin (1947) may be among the first to use gatekeeper terminology. Gatekeepers can affect decision making and even the eating habits of a group.

In the second *sample reference*, Kurtz (1968) describes a gatekeeper as a "helper [who] is a systematic link between . . . two cultures." Gatekeepers help people "gain access to resources needed to solve problems. . . ." (p. 66).

In the third *sample reference*, Metoyer-Duran (1991) studies information seeking behavior of the ethnolinguistic gatekeeper, who is:

> An individual who typically operates in two or more speech communities (one English), and who links these communities by providing information. Ethnolinguistic gatekeepers can in-

clude monolingual individuals who operate within the context of two cultures. (p. 321)

goodness of fit. How well empirical data match a theoretical or hypothetical model or mathematical expression of a bibliometric law. Statistical tools for measuring goodness of fit include the chi square technique and the Kolmogorov-Smirnov test.

'In the *sample reference*, Ajiferuke (1991) collects data from 16 abstracting journals and notes how many articles have exactly one author each, how many have two authors, how many have three authors, and so on. The writer uses the chi square statistic to test the goodness of fit of the data into 15 models. The models are probability distributions based on such bibliometric laws as Zipf's law and on such mathematical concepts as the binomial distribution.

graph. *See* **bibliograph**; **Bradford curve**.

Groos droop. Part of a bibliometric curve that droops near the end of the curve. This can transform what would have been a J-shaped curve into an S-shaped curve. The Groos droop is often associated with graphs of Bradford's law. It is named for Ole V. Groos.

The Groos droop may appear in a graph in which the vertical axis represents the cumulative number of items (usually articles), and the horizontal axis represents either the logarithm of the cumulative number of sources (usually journals) or the logarithm of the ranks of the sources.

When the data for all the articles and journals are graphed, a curve appears like the one in Exhibit 11, which is based on hypothetical data for 800 journals that produce 1,290 articles.

The Groos droop begins at about the indicated point and makes the whole curve look something like an S.

The alternative to a Groos droop is for the curve to continue on a steep, almost straight line. Exhibit 11 shows this alternative with a dashed extension of the curve. Without the Groos droop, the curve looks more like a J than an S.

The first *sample reference* is Groos' own brief report (1967) of this phenomenon.

In the second *sample reference*, Rousseau (1990a) displays a Groos droop in an analysis of articles and serials in the field of microcomputer software. He suggests that a reason for the occurrence of a Groos droop is a higher concentration than expected of articles in the most productive journals.

Similarly, a lower than expected concentration of articles in the least productive journals may also cause the droop.

growth. Usually refers to an increase in the number of documents published in a subject field. It is often called the growth of the literature of the field. A study of the growth of a literature is often considered a study of the size of the literature. See **growth rate**.

Evidence of growth includes not only an increase in documents (especially articles), but also increases in sources (especially authors and journals) of the documents. Simple measures of growth are annual counts of: documents published, documents cited, authors listed by indexing and abstracting services, or number of journal titles.

EXHIBIT 11.
The Groos droop.

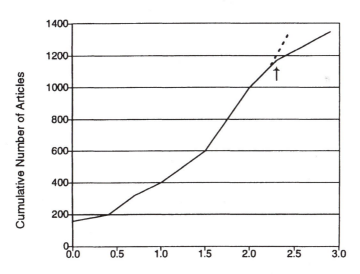

Logarithm of Cumulative Number of Journals

In the first *sample reference*, Efthimiadis (1990) examines the increasing number of publications about online public access library catalogs between 1970 and 1985.

In the second *sample reference*, Price (1965) examines the growth of science over the decades.

In the third *sample reference*, Fisher (1991) displays the growth of journals published by a professional society in endocrinology.

growth rate. In measuring the growth of the number of publications in a subject field, this is often a measure of the annual increase or decrease.

For example, if a field produces 550 articles in 1992 and 700 in 1993, then the growth rate between 1992 and 1993 is:

$$\frac{700 - 500}{550} = \frac{150}{550} = 0.27$$

Growth rate may be linear or exponential. An example of linear growth occurs in a field in which the number of documents increases by the same amount, say 50 documents, every year. This would be the case if:

250 documents are published in 1991;
300 documents are published in 1992;
350 documents are published in 1993;
400 documents are published in 1994.

A two dimensional graph of this growth is a straight line. In Exhibit 12, it is the lower line. Such a graph is represented by a linear equation, an equation in which the variable (n in this example) is not an exponent. The following linear equation represents the 50-documents per year increase example given above:

$f(n) = 50 * (n - 1991) + 250$

where:

$f(n)$ is the number of documents produced in year n.

An example of exponential growth occurs in a field in which the number of documents increases, say, 50 percent every year. This would be the case if:

250 documents are published in 1991;
250 + 125 = 375 in 1992;
375 + 187 = 562 in 1993;
562 + 281 = 843 in 1994.

A two dimensional graph of this growth is a curved line. In Exhibit 12, it is the upper line. Such a graph is represented by an exponential equation, an equation in which the variable (n in this example) is an exponent. The following exponential equation represents the 50 percent per year increase example given above:

$$f(n) = 250 * 1.50^{(n - 1991)}$$

where:

f(n) is the number of documents produced in year n.

EXHIBIT 12.
Two types of growth rates.

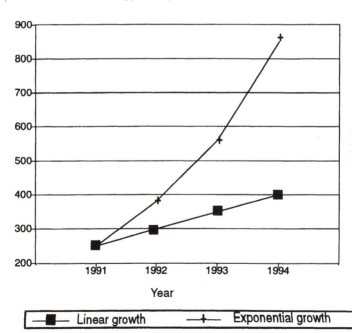

The equation for exponential growth is often expressed using the number $e = 2.71828 \ldots$ as the number associated with the exponent. The exponential equation immediately above can be rewritten using e:

$$f(n) = 250 * e^{0.405(n-1991)}$$

In the *sample reference*, Efthimiadis (1990) analyzes articles published in 1970-1985 on the topic of online public access library catalogs. The growth is exponential (about 74.4 percent per year) until about 1984. After that it seems to slow down and become linear.

H

half life. A measure of diachronous obsolescence (**obsolescence, diachronous**). It is obtained by subtracting the publication year of the source documents from the median publication year of the documents that cite the source documents.

For example, consider a group of source documents published in 1974. These might be all the articles published in a certain journal during 1974. Let the following years be the publication dates of 83 documents that cite the source documents between 1975 and 1990.

1975 (9 Citations)	1983 (7)
1976 (6)	1984 (5)
1977 (7)	1985 (7)
1978 (6)	1986 (2)
1979 (7)	1987 (5)
1980 (7)	1988 (2)
1981 (7)	1989 (2)
1982 (3)	1990 (1)

The median or middle year of the 83 dates is 1980. Then, 1980 minus 1974 equals six years. So, the half life in this analysis is six years. The exact value of the median year (and, hence, the half life) may differ depending on the statistical technique used to calculate a median.

Because half life involves calculating a median, some use half life synonymously with median citation age.

Compare with **currency**; **half life, cited**; **half life, citing**; **immediacy index**; **mean citation age**; **Price's index**; **recency score**.

In the *sample reference*, Stinson and Lancaster (1987) examine half life of the genetics literature.

half life, cited. A measure of journal use. It is published in the Institute for Scientific Information's *Journal Citation Reports®*. Cited half life is not the same as the **half life** described in the previous entry.

In the *sample reference*, *Journal Citation Reports*® itself defines cited half life as: "the number of journal publication years from the current year going back whose articles have accounted for 50% of the total citations received in a given year" (*SSCI Journal Citation Reports*, 1988, p. 23A).

Compare this definition with the definition for citing half life (**half life**, **citing**) in the next entry. The crucial difference is the phrase "received in a given year" in the current definition instead of "given . . . during the current year" in the next entry's definition. The *sample reference* above gives a detailed example of cited half life on the same page as its definition.

One may not have to calculate cited half life, because *Journal Citation Reports*® annually lists the cited half lives for journals in its editions that accompany *Arts & Humanities Citation Index*®, *Science Citation Index*®, and *Social Sciences Citation Index*®.

When a writer says "half life" without qualifying it, then the writer is probably referring to half life in the sense of the previous entry. Unfortunately, some people use half life synonymously with a related but not identical term, median citation age.

Compare with **currency**; **immediacy index**; **mean citation age**; **Price's index**; **recency score**.

half life, **citing**. A measure of journal use. It is published in the Institute for Scientific Information's *Journal Citation Reports*®.

In the *sample reference*, *Journal Citation Reports*® itself defines citing half life as: "the number of journal publication years from the current year going back which account for 50% of the total citations given by the citing journal during the current year" (*SSCI Journal Citation Reports*, 1988, p. 22A).

Compare with cited half life (**half life**, **cited**). The crucial difference is the phrase "given by the citing journal during the current year" in the current definition instead of "received in a given year" in the previous definition. The *sample reference* above gives a detailed example of citing half life on the same page as its definition.

One may not have to calculate citing half life because *Journal Citation Reports*® annually lists the citing half lives for journals in its editions that accompany *Arts & Humanities Citation Index*®, *Science Citation Index*®, and *Social Sciences Citation Index*®.

When a writer says "half life" without qualifying it, then the writer is probably referring to half life in the sense of the entry labeled simply: half life. Unfortunately, some people use half life synonymously with median citation age.

Compare with **currency; immediacy index; mean citation age; Price's index; recency score**.

halo effect. *See* **citation, biased; Matthew effect**.

hard science. *See* **science, hard and soft**.

hidden self citation. *See* **self citation, hidden**.

hot topic index. A measure of how trendy the topic of an article is or will be. Its calculation is based on the recency and the size of the article's collection of references. The hot topic index is obtained by dividing the density ratio of a document by its recency score.

In the *sample reference*, Kidd (1990) develops the hot topic index to help identify the emergence of a potentially important research topic.

I

immediacy index. A measure of how quickly a group of documents, usually articles in a journal, receives citations to itself.

For example, consider the calculation of the immediacy index for all 1994 issues of a certain journal. The journal's immediacy index is the following ratio:

$$\frac{\text{the number of citations received by the journal in 1994 to the articles published by the journal in 1994}}{\text{the number of articles published by the journal in 1994}}$$

In particular, assume that:

Journal A publishes 20 articles in 1994;
    these articles receive 1 citation during 1994;
Journal B publishes 20 articles in 1994;
    these articles receive 5 citations during 1994;
Journal C publishes 240 articles in 1994;
    these articles receive 12 citations during 1994.

Then, the immediacy indexes for 1994 for the three journals are:

Journal A: $1/20 = 0.05$;
Journal B: $5/20 = 0.25$;
Journal C: $12/240 = 0.05$.

The citations to journals A, B, and C would come from a collection of journals to be analyzed. This collection typically includes A, B, C, and other journals in the same subject field as A, B, and C.

Note that the ratio for the immediacy index of a journal looks similar to the ratio for the impact factor of a journal. In fact, the immediacy index is the impact factor, too, but with the stipulation that the citations be received during the same year that the cited articles are published.

Immediacy index data for journals are available in various editions of the Institute for Scientific Information's *Journal Citation Reports*®.

Compare with **currency, half life, mean citation age, median citation age, Price's index,** and **recency score.**

In the first *sample reference*, Garfield (1986b), the developer of the immediacy index and other citation measures, reports the immediacy index for journals in general and internal medicine.

In the second *sample reference*, Sievert and Haughawout (1989) compare three editorships of a journal by determining the immediacy index and other bibliometric indicators for each of the time periods.

impact. A measure of the importance or influence of a document or group of documents.

In its simpler form, impact is the number of citations received by the document or group during a specified period. In this sense, it can be used synonymously with citation rate.

In its more complex form, it is actually what some call the impact factor, a ratio that compares the number of citations received by a group of documents to the number of documents in the group. Impact factor is probably a more appropriate term than impact when talking about this ratio.

In the *sample reference*, Peritz (1983) compares impact (number of citations received) to scholarliness (number of citations listed in a bibliography) for documents in sociology.

impact factor. A measure of the importance or influence of a group of documents. Speaking imprecisely, impact factor is the number of citations received by an average document in the group. Speaking more precisely, the impact factor is the following ratio:

$$\frac{\text{Number of citations received by the documents}}{\text{Number of documents in the group}}$$

For example, one can examine the impact factor of a journal. Then, the group of documents are all the articles published in the journal during a given period. In particular, assume that:

Journal A publishes 20 articles in 1993-94;
   these articles receive 15 citations during 1993-94;
Journal B publishes 20 articles in 1993-1994;
   these articles receive 50 citations during 1993-94;

Journal C publishes 240 articles in 1993-94;
   these articles receive 300 citations during 1993-94.

Then, the impact factors for the given time periods for the three journals are:

Journal A: 15/20 = 0.75;
Journal B: 50/20 = 2.50;
Journal C: 300/240 = 1.25.

This means, for example, that journal C receives, on average, about 1.25 citations for each of its articles during the given time period.

The citations to journals A, B, and C come from a collection of journals to be analyzed. This collection typically includes A, B, C, and other journals in the same subject field as A, B, and C.

When calculating impact factors, one may decide to use a range of years larger or smaller than the two year range used in the above example.

Annual impact factors for many journals are listed in various editions of the Institute for Scientific Information's *Journal Citation Reports®*.

Impact factor is also called **journal impact factor, journal influence, citation rate**, or **impact**. However, the two latter terms are most appropriately used to mean how many citations a document or group of documents receives during a given period.

Compare with **immediacy index, importance index, influence weight, standing**.

In the first *sample reference*, Garfield (1972) describes the introduction of the impact factor as a device to balance the effect of the size of a journal on the number of citations it receives.

In the second *sample reference*, Nederhof and Noyons (1992) calculate impact factors for the publications of the academic departments that they are comparing.

In the third *sample reference*, Moline (1991) examines the correlation between impact factor and the cents per thousand characters statistic for mathematics journals.

In the fourth *sample reference*, Fisher (1991) describes impact factors for journals in endocrinology.

impact factor, author. A type of impact factor calculated for the documents produced by a single author. A simple version of the author impact factor is the number of citations received by the author's documents divided by the number of documents published by the author.

A more complex way to calculate the author impact factor is to use the impact factors of the journals in which the author has published. For example, if the author has published three documents in journal A, two in journal B, and four in journal C, then the author's impact factor is:

$$3 * I_A + 2 * I_B + 4 * I_C$$

where:

I_A, I_B, and I_C are the impact factors of journals A, B, and C, respectively.

One would have to decide whether to use the same or different years when recording the impact factors for the various journals and whether to find the average of $3*I_A$, $2*I_B$, and $4*I_C$.

In the *sample reference*, Beck and Gaspar (1991) use author impact factor and other measures to evaluate the research performance of faculty members.

impact factor, discipline. A measure that can be used to identify the importance of core journals in a discipline. The discipline impact factor (DIF) is like the better known impact factor. Unlike the usual impact factor, the DIF requires that one start out knowing (or taking a good guess at) the identity of at least one journal with a high impact factor in the discipline.

In the first *sample reference*, Hirst (1978) introduces the DIF, saying that it:

> measures the number of times a paper in a journal is cited in the core literature of the given discipline. This definition is, of course, circular: A knowledge of the core journals is required to determine the core journals. (p. 171)

The DIF is an iterative measure. Here is an example.

First, identify one or a few journals that are clearly important to that discipline. These journals are called the citing set.

Second, select another journal whose importance you are not sure about. To test it as a possible core journal, calculate the discipline impact factor of this candidate journal. For some time period, the DIF is the following ratio:

$$\frac{\text{the number of citations from the journal(s) in the citing set to articles in the candidate journal}}{\text{the number of articles in the candidate journal}}$$

There is no rule for the time period to be covered. One possibility is to use 1993-95 for the numerator of the DIF and 1991-93 for the denominator.

Third, if the candidate journal's DIF is greater than some threshold, it is added to the citing set.

Fourth and fifth, test a new candidate journal, redoing steps two and three.

Continue this procedure until the citing set does not change very much, if at all.

It is possible to subtract journals from the citing set during this procedure, if one starts with a journal or group of journals that turn out not to be core journals.

In the second *sample reference*, Hirst and Talent (1977) give an example of the DIF using computer science journals. For 50 journals tested, 21 fall into a core that has a DIF threshold of 0.050 (p. 235).

impact factor, expected. A type of impact factor calculated for a group of articles collected from many journals. For example, these may be all the articles on a given topic published during a specified period of time. The expected impact factor for the group of articles is the average (mean) impact factors of the journals in which they appear. Also called **expected citation rate**.

In the *sample reference*, Braun and Schubert (1991) graph actual impact factors versus expected impact factors for groups of scientific articles published in various countries.

impact factor, journal. *See* **impact factor**.

importance. The tendency of a document or author to be cited by other documents or authors. An assumption is that more important documents or authors get cited more than do the less important ones.

A similar quality is influence, but influence usually refers to the tendency for one particular item to cite another. It is then said that the cited item has influence over the citing item.

Compare the informal idea of importance with the formal measures of **impact factor, importance index, influence weight**.

importance index. A measure of the relative importance of one journal among a group of journals in a given subject area. The basic evidence of importance is how often articles in the journal cite and are cited. Compare with **impact factor, influence weight, standing**.

Calculating the importance index usually means that one is analyzing a group of journals and has collected data on how often they cite each other. The data are put into a citation matrix.

In the first *sample reference*, Salancik (1986) derives the importance index and uses it to compare two journals in applied psychology. The journals are considered "members" of a group of journals in the field. Using that terminology, the importance index of a journal is "proportional to the dependencies of others [other members or journals] on the member and their importance and the member's own intrinsic importance" (p. 200).

In the second *sample reference*, Kim (1992, p. 81) calculates the importance index for nine library and information science journals. The importance index from journal A to journal B during a given time period is the following ratio:

$$\frac{\text{the number of citations from journal A to journal B}}{\begin{array}{c}\text{the number of citations from journal A to all}\\\text{documents, whether or not they are in the}\\\text{group being analyzed}\end{array}}$$

For example, let us use the above ratio and assume we are analyzing a group of three journals, A, B, and C. Assume articles in journal A have cited articles in journal B 15 times during the period being studied. Count all the citations listed in the articles in journal A during this time. Assume that there are 200 such citations: 125 to articles in journals A, B, and C, and 75 to other documents. Then the importance index of journal A to journal B is:

$$\frac{15}{200} = 0.075$$

In a complete analysis, the importance index of one journal may be expressed as an average of the importance indexes of the journal with each of the others.

index coverage. *See* **coverage**; **coverage overlap**.

indicator. *See* **bibliometric indicator**; **science indicator**.

inequality. The idea that some entities are richer than others. Also called **concentration**. Compare with **dispersion, diversity**.

In bibliometrics, we see inequality, for example, in analyses of Lotka's law, when only a few authors are prolific and many others produce only one or two publications each.

The concept of inequality may be borrowed from economics, which studies inequalities among peoples and nations.

In the *sample reference*, Atkinson (1970) says that economists commonly use measures of inequality to answer questions like: "Is the distribution of income more equal than it was in the past? Are underdeveloped countries characterised by greater inequality than advanced countries?" (p. 244).

influence. The tendency of an author, document, or journal to be cited by another author, document, or journal. The cited item is said to have influence over the citing item. The citing item is said to have receptivity for the cited item.

Also called **impact, impact factor, importance**. Compare the informal meaning of influence with the formal measure of **influence weight**.

In the *sample reference*, Everett and Pecotich (1991) examine a model of citations between journals based on influence and receptivity. In this model, the influence of a cited journal on a citing journal is calculated as the product of the cited journal's importance times the similarity between the two journals.

influence weight. A measure of the relative influence of one journal among a group of journals in a given subject area. The basic evidence of influence is how often articles in the journal cite and are cited. Compare with the **impact factor, importance index, standing**.

Calculating the influence weight usually means that one is analyzing a group of journals and has collected data on how often they cite each other. The data are put into a citation matrix.

In the first *sample reference*, Pinski and Narin (1976) develop this measure and say it is a "size independent measure of the weighted number of citations a journal receives from the other journals, normalized by the number of references it gives to other journals" (p. 298).

In the second *sample reference*, Kim (1992, p. 81) calculates the influence weight for nine library and information science journals. The influence weight from journal A to journal B during a given time period is the following ratio:

$$\frac{\text{the number of citations from journal A to journal B}}{\substack{\text{the number of citations from journal B to} \\ \text{all the journals in the group being analyzed}}}$$

Using the above ratio, assume the analysis involves three journals that produce the citation matrix in Exhibit 13. Then the influence weight from journal A to journal B is:

$$\frac{8}{12} = 0.667$$

In a complete analysis, the influence weight of one journal may be expressed as an average of the influence weights of the journal with each of the others.

informal communication. *See* **communication, informal.**

informatics. A term that has meant both the (1) application of science to the study and delivery of information, as well as (2) the study of the use of information in the sciences. In the first sense, it may be a synonym for information science. In the second sense, it can include scientometrics and scholarly communication. Informatics at times also comes close to being synonymous with the terms information technology and computer science.

The first *sample reference* demonstrates that the term has encompassed many aspects, including information storage and retrieval, scholarly communication, and scientometrics.

[I]t appears that informatics emerged on the international scene as an independent discipline in the late forties–early fifties of this century.

The subject matter of informetrics are processes, methods and laws related to the recording, analytical-synthetical processing, storage, retrieval, and dissemination of scientific information. . . . (Mikhailov, Chernyi, and Gilyarevskii, 1969, pp. 13-14)

In the second *sample reference*, Schrader (1983) describes the link of informatics with information science and with information technology:

It was in the context of computers, mathematical information theory, cybernetics, operations research, and other quantitative approaches to behavioral and social phenomena that the American term "information science" first appeared publicly in 1959, . . . and that the Russian term "informatics" was first suggested in 1962 by Kharkevich in a letter to Mikhailov, as a designation for the discipline of scientific information. . . . (pp. 120-121)

EXHIBIT 13.
A citation matrix for calculating influence weights.

Citing Journals

		A	B	C	Total
	A	15	7	20	42
Cited					
	B	8	2	12	22
Journals					
	C	7	3	5	15
	Total	30	12	37	79

Today, the term seems to be more focused, in that it includes information technology more than any of the other elements listed in the definition above. At the same time, it may be used in any situation, not only in studying the sciences, in which information technology plays a role.

The third *sample reference* demonstrates that the term today can be taken out of academia and moved into the home.

> The term "Home Informatics" refers to the applications of Information Technology (IT) products that are emerging for use by members of private households. It covers not only items of *hardware, . . .* but also both the *software* that programmes this equipment, the *services . . .* that may be used with the hardware and software, and the *networks* or systems that are formed by linking together groups of users. (Miles, 1988, p. 1)

information production process. An activity in which information is produced. Many bibliometric laws involve such processes, and so this concept provides a demonstration of what they have in common. Depending on the subject field, the process may involve activities studied by bibliometricians, econometricians, informetricians, linguists, and others.

In the *sample reference*, Egghe (1990a) introduces the term and gives it a formal mathematical definition. The writer also provides examples of information production processes such as the following:

> profit or salary produced by workers;
> population of people produced by cities;
> words produced by texts;
> articles produces by journals.

In both the mathematical definition and verbal examples, Egghe (1990a) uses the terminology of items and sources. For example, when we say that a journal produces articles, the journal is a source, and the articles are items.

informetrics. Sometimes used synonymously with bibliometrics, but considered by some to cover a larger area than bibliometrics. In the latter situation, informetrics includes all of bibliometrics as well as the mathematical and statistical analysis of bibliometric-like patterns found in other areas of life.

For example, Willis' law on the relationship between the age and geographic area covered by species, and Pareto's law on the allocation of wealth to members of a community may be informetric but not bibliometric laws, because Willis' and Pareto's laws do not deal directly with publication patterns. Bradford's law on the scatter of articles among journals may be considered both informetric and bibliometric. When Bradford's law is used to analyze research and publication patterns in science, then the law is also part of scientometrics.

In the first *sample reference*, Rousseau (1990b) uses bibliometrics and informetrics synonymously: "Bibliometric (or informetric) research has developed a rich body of theoretical knowledge, which in turn aims at finding wider applications in all practical aspects of information work. . . ." (p. 197).

In the second *sample reference*, Bookstein (1990) is discussing informetric distributions or regularities, such as Bradford's law, Lotka's law, Pareto's law, and Zipf's law:

> Terminology varies here. There is some confusion regarding the use of the terms *Informetrics, Bibliometrics,* and *Scientometrics.* In earlier papers I referred to the regularities discussed here as the *Bibliometric* regularities. My impression is that this term is being replaced in the literature by *Informetrics,* a term suggesting a wider range of applicability, and my usage in this paper is intended to be consistent with this evolution. (p. 368)

Later on in the second *sample reference*, Bookstein (1990) notes a commonality among informetric patterns, laws, or, in his words, "regularities:"

> These regularities usually start with a population of discrete entities, for example, businessmen, scientists, words, or journals. Each of these entities is *producing* something over a time-like variable–dollars earned, articles published, occurrences of articles in a given discipline. . . . (p. 369)

In the third *sample reference*, Egghe (1988a) says that "[v]ery exceptionally one sees also the term 'Informetrics' . . . and even 'Librametrics' . . . , but they are not widespread" (p. 180).

In the fourth *sample reference*, Egghe and Rousseau (1990) suggest:

> In our view, informetrics deals with the measurement, hence also the mathematical theory and modelling of all aspects of information and the storage and retrieval of information. It is mathematical meta-information, i.e. a theory of information on information, scientifically developed with the aid of mathematical tools. . . . (p. 1)

Also in the fourth *sample reference*, Egghe and Rousseau (1990) present a diagram in which bibliometrics and scientometrics are two of the several components of informetrics (p. 3).

Compare informetrics with the definition of a word that has a similar spelling: **informatics**.

innovator. Characterization of a person as someone who devises new ways to do things. Some writers in scientometrics and scholarly communication study innovators, as well as adaptors and adopters.

In the first *sample reference*, Palmer (1991) uses the Kirton adaption innovation theory as a basis for contrasting scientists as innovators or adapters.

In the second *sample reference*, an entire issue of a journal is devoted to papers on failed innovations, that is, innovations that are not successful at the time and place of their introduction. An example is the electric plow in pre-World War I Germany (Braun, 1992).

interjournal citation. *See* **citation, interjournal**.

internal citation. *See* **citation, internal**.

intrajournal citation. *See* **citation, intrajournal**.

inverse exponential law. *See* **inverse square law; Lotka's Law**.

inverse square law. A name sometimes applied to Lotka's law because one version of the Lotka formula may be expressed as:

$$x^2y = c \text{ or } y = c/x^2 \text{ or } y = cx^{-2}$$

where:

y is the fraction of authors making x contributions each to a collection of documents on a given subject;

c is a parameter that depends on the field being analyzed.

invisible college. A group of scholars, scientists, or other professionals who share a common scholarly or professional interest. The college is "invisible" in the sense that it is without walls and includes everyone who shares the interest regardless of their location in the world. For some investigators, a criterion for membership in the college is not only a common interest but also communication among other members.

Workers in bibliometrics, scholarly communication, and scientometrics make a college less invisible by examining communication, especially informal communication (**communication, informal**), among college members. Examples of communication are citations, electronic mail, speeches, and telephone messages. One way of displaying communication in an invisible college is to draw a sociogram. The sociogram is a diagram that indicates who communicates with whom. Sometimes the diagram also shows how often the communication takes place.

A sociogram may show that the college is divided into groups that tend to communicate more within their group than with other groups. The sociogram may also identify individuals who receive and send many more communications than the typical college member.

In the first *sample reference*, the subjects are rural sociologists specializing in the investigation of the diffusion of agricultural innovations. Crane (1969) uses a questionnaire to collect data on informal communication among the sociologists.

In the second *sample reference*, Crawford (1971) examines informal communication among sleep researchers. Display of the results includes several sociograms.

items and sources. The entities that are analyzed by the major bibliometric laws (such as Bradford's law, Lotka's law, and Zipf's law.) For example, in a Bradford analysis, the items are often journal articles, and the sources are then the journals that produce the articles. Also called **sources and items**.

Item and source terminology allows one to speak generally (rather than in terms of documents) when describing bibliometric or informetric patterns. In a Lotka analysis (**Lotka's law**), the sources are authors, and the items are documents that the authors produce. In Zipf's law, the sources are the text, or more precisely the rank of words in the text, and the items are the number of occurrences that each ranked word produces. In Willis' law, the sources are genera of organisms, and the items are the species they produce.

The writer of the first *sample reference* may be a major encourager for the use of this terminology, especially for Bradford analyses (Brookes, 1977).

In the second *sample reference*, Rorick (1987) describes an analysis of recordings of the symphonies of Ludwig van Beethoven. Although items and sources are not mentioned, the symphonies are the sources and the recordings are the items. For example, Beethoven's symphony number five produces the most items (153 recordings), while symphony number two produces the least (86 recordings).

J

joint authorship. *See* **authorship, multiple.**

journal, attraction power. *See* **attraction power of a journal.**

journal citation factor. *See* **citation factor.**

Journal Citation Reports®. A publication of the Institute for Scientific Information. An annual edition appears for each of three services: Arts & Humanities Citation Index®, Science Citation Index®, and Social Sciences Citation Index®.
  Each edition provides bibliometric data for journals, including: number of citations received, cited half life (**half life, cited**), citing half life (**half life, citing**), impact factor, and immediacy index.

journal citations. *See* **citation factor; cocitation; consumption factor; half life, cited; half life, citing; impact factor; popularity factor.**

journal citation speed. *See* **mean response time.**

journal cocitation analysis. *See* **cocitation analysis, journal.**

journal consumption factor. *See* **consumption factor.**

journal, core. *See* **core journal.**

journal coverage. *See* **coverage; coverage overlap.**

journal half life. *See* **half life, cited; half life, citing.**

journal impact factor. *See* **impact factor.**

journal importance. *See* **importance index.**

journal influence. *See* **influence weight.**

journal, peripheral. *See* **peripheral journal.**

journal popularity factor. *See* **popularity factor.**

journal standing. *See* **standing.**

journal to journal citation. *See* **citation, interjournal; citation matrix.**

junior author. *See* **author, secondary.**

K

Kirton adaption innovation theory. The idea that individuals, especially as members of organizations, are either adaptors or innovators or have characteristics of both. The theory is of interest to researchers in scholarly communication and scientometrics, in their examinations of how scholars and scientists communicate with their colleagues. The theory is named for psychologist Michael Kirton.

In the first *sample reference*, Kirton (1976) says:

> The contention . . . is that everyone can be located on a continuum ranging from an ability to "do things better" to an ability to "do things differently," and the ends of the continuum are labeled *adaptive* and *innovative*, respectively. (p. 622)

In the second *sample reference*, Palmer (1991) uses the Kirton adaption innovation theory as a basis for contrasting scientists as innovators or adapters.

Kolmogorov-Smirnov test. A statistical test that (in its two-sample form), compares the distribution of the populations from which two independent samples are drawn. It can also compare a theoretical distribution with an observed distribution. The test is sometimes called a goodness of fit test, and it occurs in some tests of the laws of bibliometrics, as well in tests of models in mathematics and other fields.

In the first *sample reference*, Freed, Hess, and Ryan (1989, p. 407) give the formula as:

$D = \text{Maximum } |F_1(X) - F_2(X)|$

where:

$F_1(X)$ is the cumulative frequency distribution for the first sample at the corresponding value of X;

$F_2(X)$ is the cumulative frequency distribution for the second sample at the corresponding value of X;

| | is the absolute value operation.

In the second *sample reference*, Cook (1989, 1991) uses the Kolmogorov-Smirnov test to determine how well observed data for the production of musical hits by artists compare with theoretical data from Lotka's law and Bradford's law.

In the third *sample reference*, Budd and Seavey (1990) use the Kolmogorov-Smirnov test to evaluate Lotka's law as a description of authorship patterns in librarianship.

L

lag time. *See* **time lag, citation; time lag, indexing; time lag, publishing**.

law. Eponymic statements in bibliometrics, informetrics, and scientometrics.

Law may be a misleading and even sloppy designation. Many of the laws have variants. The algebraic expression of a law may change, depending on who is describing it. A law may have several components, and it is not always clear which piece of the law someone is discussing.

The laws are descriptions or hypotheses about patterns that seem to be common in the publication and use of information. They are not the formal, highly validated laws we associate with the physical sciences.

Among the best known laws of bibliometrics, informetrics, and scientometrics are:

Booth's law;
Bradford's law;
Brookes' law;
Estroup's law;
Leimkuhler's law;
Lotka's law;
Pareto's law;
Price's law;
Willis' law;
Zipf's law.

In the *sample reference*, Zunde (1984) describes some of these laws in a discussion on the foundations of information science.

least effort, principle of. *See* **principle of least effort**.

least publishable unit. A cynical term that refers to the practice by some authors of publishing a research report in as many pieces as possible to increase their number of publications. This is also known as fragmentation and paper inflation.

In the first *sample reference*, Broad (1981) notes the contribution of this practice to the growth of the literature of science.

In the second *sample reference*, Schwartz (1992) briefly describes the least publishable unit in an essay on significant research versus routine research.

Leimkuhler's law. A bibliometric law that describes the number of items (such as articles) produced by a number of sources (such as journals). The law is named for Ferdinand F. Leimkuhler (b. 1928). Compare with **Bradford's law, Brookes' law**.

For a given subject field over a given period of time, collect all the items published. List the sources in rank order, with the most prolific listed first. Then, one version of Leimkuhler's law is:

$$R(r) = a * \ln(1 + br),$$

where:

R(r) is the number of items produced cumulatively by the sources of ranks 1 through r;
a and b are parameters that depend on the subject field;
ln is the natural *logarithm*.

For example, if the top three journals in a field produce 500 articles during a certain time, then $r = 3$, and $R(r) = R(3) = 500$.

The first *sample reference* describes this version of the law (Rousseau, 1990b, p. 198).

Another version of Leimkuhler's law expresses the same concept in terms of fractions:

$$F(x) = \frac{\ln(1 + Bx)}{\ln(1 + B),}$$

where:

F(x) is the fraction of items produced (compared to all items produced) by the first sources of ranks 1 through x;
x is a fraction of all the sources;

B is a parameter that depends on the subject field;
ln is the natural logarithm.

For example, if the top three journals produce 500 articles and the entire analysis examined 60 journals that produced 5,000 articles, then, x = 3/60 = 0.05, and F(x) = F(0.05) = 500/5,000 = 0.10.

This version of Leimkuhler's law is produced by Leimkuhler (1967) and is in the second *sample reference* (p. 206).

literature, primary. A subject field's documents, usually articles, that may be indexed by an indexing and abstracting service sometime after publication.

Some people feel that both articles and books are part of a field's primary literature. However, others may argue that the rapidity with which an article is published compared with a book makes the information in the article more primary than the information in a book.

The important distinction is between primary literature and secondary literature (**literature, secondary**). Some writers also discuss tertiary literature (**literature, tertiary**).

literature, secondary. The indexes that provide access to the primary literature (**literature, primary**) of a field. Some writers also discuss tertiary literature (**literature, tertiary**).

literature, tertiary. An infrequently used term that logically (after primary literature and secondary literature) should be an index or bibliography of indexes to articles in a subject field.

However, one could argue that publications that integrate new primary literature into the established literature of a field comprise the tertiary literature. Examples of such integrating publications are annual reviews and textbooks.

More important is the distinction between primary literature (**literature, primary**) and secondary literature (**literature, secondary**).

logarithm. A mathematical operation frequently used in bibliometric analyses. Users of logarithms usually employ either the common logarithm or the natural logarithm.

BASIC INFORMATION

The common logarithm of a number, x, is the exponent needed to raise 10 to the number x. This may be written as:

$\log_{10}x$

If x is 100, then $\log_{10}100$ is 2, because 10^2 is 100.

If x is 52, then $\log_{10}52$ is about 1.72, because $10^{1.72}$ is about 52.

The natural logarithm of a number, x, is the exponent needed to raise the number e (2.71828 . . .) to the number x. This may be written as:

$\log_{e}x$ or ln x

If x is 100, then ln 100 is about 4.61 because $e^{4.61}$ is about 100.

If x is 52, then ln 52 is about 3.95 because $e^{3.95}$ is about 52.

Sometimes writers simply write the logarithm symbol without the "10" or "e" or "n" symbol, as in log 15. This probably means the common logarithm of 15, but the reader should look for an indication in the text of the document being read.

INCONSISTENT USE OF COMMON AND NATURAL LOGARITHMS

One may find that some writers use common logarithms and natural logarithms in the same article. It is also possible to find that one writer uses common logarithms to describe or test a certain concept, perhaps Bradford's law, while another writer uses natural logarithms for the same concept.

In the *sample reference*, Drott and Griffith (1978) give an explanation for some of this inconsistency: "There seems to be some tendency in the literature to use common logarithms when employing graphical methods but to switch to natural (base *e*) logarithms when solving algebraically" (p. 240).

LOGARITHMS AND GRAPHS

Logarithms are sometimes useful when displaying graphs. This is because: (1) logarithms transform some otherwise curved lines into straight lines; (2) logarithms allow data with large frequencies to fit on a relatively small graph.

For example, Exhibit 14a and Exhibit 14b are pictures of the data from which Bradford's law developed. The data come from the second *sample reference*, in which Bradford (1934) collects data about journals and articles in the field of applied geophysics:

> the top ranked journal produces 93 articles;
> the top 2 journals together produce 179 articles;
> the top 3 journals together produce 235 articles;
>   and so on until
> the top 108 journals together produce 1065 articles;
> the top 157 journals together produce 1163 articles;
> the top 326 journals together produce 1332 articles.

EXHIBIT 14a.
A semi-log graph.

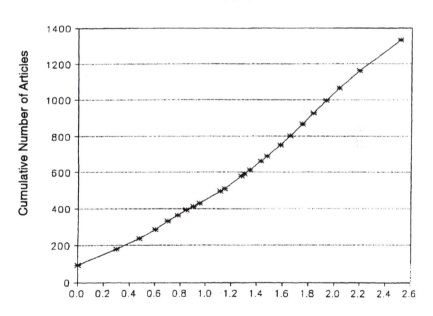

Log of Cumulative Number of Journals

EXHIBIT 14b.
A log-log graph.

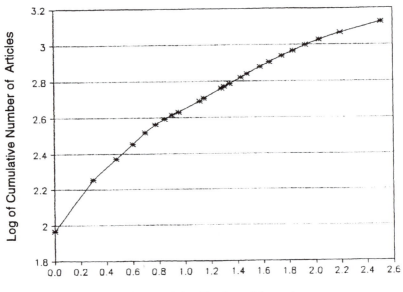

Log of Cumulative Number of Journals

Exhibit 14a is an example of a semi-log graph, a graph where logarithms are used on only one of the axes. In this case the horizontal axis in Exhibit 14a plots the common logarithm of 1, 2, 3, . . . , 108, 157, and 326. The vertical axis plots the article numbers 93, 179, 235, . . . , 1065, 1163, and 1332. Note that using logarithms allows all the points for the journals to appear, even though they range from 1 to 326 (before using the logarithms). And note that the graph is close to being a straight line; it would be much more of a curve if logarithms had not been used.

Exhibit 14b is an example of a log-log graph, where common logarithms are used on both axes of a graph. In this case, the horizontal axis represents the same data as for the horizontal axis of Exhibit 14a. But the vertical axis of Exhibit 14b is the common logarithm of the number of articles.

Some graphs use logarithms indirectly. This occurs when the horizontal or vertical marks on the graph are printed at logarithmic distances. Using Bradford's data, that would mean we could plot the journals numbers (1, 2, 3, . . . , 108, 157, and 326) directly onto the graph without calculating logarithms. But the graph marks would be arranged so that the distance between 1 and 10, for example, is the same as the distance **between 10 and 100.**

Lotka's constants or **Lotka's parameters**. The n and the c (sometimes capitalized, C) in the equation of Lotka's law:

$$x^n y = c$$

The equation is explained in the following entry on Lotka's law.

Using n and c as parameters emphasizes the idea that Lotka's law is a general law that can be applied to many fields and collections of documents and their authors. Each application may have its own values of n and c.

In the *sample reference*, Pao (1986) examines 48 tests of author productivity data and reports the values and n and c for each.

Lotka's inverse square law. See **Lotka's law.**

Lotka's law. One of the major laws of bibliometrics. In a well defined subject field over a given period of time, Lotka's law suggests that a few authors are prolific and account for a relatively large percent of the publications in the field. Many other authors produce only one or two publications each. Another way to say this is that there is an inverse relation between the number of documents produced and the number of authors producing the documents.

BASIC INFORMATION

The law is named for demographer and statistician Alfred J. Lotka (1880-1949), who is the writer in the first *sample reference*. He states the following general formula:

$$x^n y = c$$

where:

y is the portion of authors making x contributions each;
n and c are parameters that depend on the field being analyzed.

Lotka (1926) examines publications in chemistry and physics for the late nineteenth and early twentieth centuries. For chemistry he finds the parameter c = 0.5669 for n = 1.888. For physics, he obtains c = 0.6079 for n = 2.02.

AN EXAMPLE

In the second *sample reference*, Keenan (1988), perhaps unwittingly, collects data that demonstrates the basic pattern of Lotka's law. For the fortieth anniversary of the *Journal of Finance*, the writer reports that during 1946-1986, "[o]ver 1800 different individuals have authored papers in the Journal. For most of them, it is a once-in-a-lifetime event" (p. 772). In particular:

1237 authors (67.1 percent of 1844) produced 1 article each;
 295 authors (16.0 percent) produced 2 articles each;
 140 authors (7.6 percent) produced 3 articles each;
  63 authors (3.4 percent) produced 4 articles each;
  41 authors (2.2 percent) produced 5 articles each;
  68 authors (3.7 percent) produced 6 or more articles each.

Out of the total 1,844 authors, only a few are prolific, and, indeed, most do write one article each. This satisfies the verbal expression of Lotka's law. To apply the data to the equation $x^n y = c$, we can transform each of the first five lines of data above into an equation with, say, n = 2, using decimals for the percents:

$$1^2 * 0.671 = 0.671$$
$$2^2 * 0.160 = 0.640$$
$$3^2 * 0.076 = 0.684$$
$$4^2 * 0.034 = 0.544$$
$$5^2 * 0.022 = 0.550$$

In this simple example, the value of c seems to be somewhere between 0.544 and 0.684. In fact, the first three values given here

(0.671, 0.640, 0.684) are similar to each other and to the values of c that Lotka himself obtained.

OTHER FORMS OF THE LAW

Because the parameter n (also known as the exponent n) is close to two in Lotka's own data, his law is sometimes called the inverse square law. Also called **inverse exponential law**. The following expressions of Lotka's law emphasize the inverse concept:

$x^2y = c$ or $y = c/x^2$ or $y = cx^{-2}$
(where y is the portion of authors making x contributions each, and c is a parameter that depends on the field being analyzed).

The third *sample reference* employs a generalized form of the law:

$g(x) = k/x^b$

where:

$g(x)$ is the portion of authors contributing x publications each;
b and k are parameters that depend on the field being tested.
(Kinnucan and Wolfram, 1990, p. 781)

TESTING THE LAW

Since about 1970, many writers have examined the applicability of Lotka's law beyond the documents he tested. In the fourth *sample reference*, Nicholls (1989) lists 30 studies that test the law against many sets of documents and authors.

In the fifth *sample reference*, Budd and Seavey (1990) identify the most prolific authors who are also college or university librarians. They use their data to test Lotka's law.

In the sixth *sample reference* Burnham, Shearer, and Wall (1992) determine that only 0.44 percent of authors of 679 articles on the topic of gaits found in a compact disc MEDLINE database account for 10 percent of the articles; these are the most prolific authors. On the other hand, almost all (about 94 percent) of the authors of the 679 articles have written no more than one or two articles each on gaits (p. 155).

COUNTING THE AUTHORS

Counting multiple authorships can complicate an analysis of Lotka's law. In such cases, there are three ways to count authorship: adjusted count, complete count, and straight count.

M

Margalef diversity index. A measure of the variety of organisms in a geographic area. It is named for biologist D. Ramon Margalef. Compare with **Willis' law**.

The Margalef diversity index is of interest to bibliometricians because it is similar to bibliometric laws like Bradford's law. For example, we can think of animal or plant species as analogous to journal articles. Then the geographic areas they live in correspond to journals. Bradford's law describes how articles are scattered among journals; similarly, the Margalef index describes how species are spread among geographic areas.

In the first *sample reference*, Margalef (1958) presents the index, which is based on the "presumed linear relation between the number of species and the logarithm of the area or the number of individuals" (p. 49). The index is:

$$d = \frac{S - 1}{\ln N}$$

where:

d is the diversity index;
S is the number of species;
ln is the natural logarithm;
N is the number of individual organisms.

In the second *sample reference*, Kelland (1990) uses this index to describe the diversity of citations in biochemistry and ecology. The number of species in the above formula becomes the number of formats of the citations (journal article, chapter in a book, thesis, patent, and so on); the number of organisms becomes the number of citations.

mathematical function. See **distribution; model**.

Matthew effect. The success-breeds-success or the-rich-get-richer phenomenon. In scholarship this occurs when already well-known individuals receive disproportionately high recognition for their new work compared to the relatively low recognition received by lesser known colleagues who do comparable work. The rewards may be grant money, prizes, honors, or citations. Also called **halo effect**. Compare with **cumulative advantage**. The Matthew effect may result in inappropriate or biased citations (**citation, biased**).

In the first *sample reference*, Merton (1968) introduces the term and applies it to science:

> [T]he Matthew effect consists in the accruing of greater increments of recognition for particular scientific contributions to scientists of considerable repute and the withholding of such recognition from scientists who have not yet made their mark. (p. 58)

Merton explains that "Matthew" alludes to a passage from the Gospel According to St. Matthew: "For unto every one that hath shall be given, and he shall have abundance; but from him that hath not shall be taken away from that which he hath" (quoted by Merton, 1968, p. 58).

In the second *sample reference*, Bensman (1985) suggests that we take the Matthew effect into account in the collection management of journals. Strong use of a journal may allow us to predict that it will receive continued use:

> [A]cademic libraries should establish systems for constantly monitoring both their external and internal journal usage in order to take advantage of the Matthew Effect. If a journal is being continually requested through interlibrary loan, it should be placed on subscription regardless of the number of other libraries holding it. (p. 25)

May's correction. A mathematical adjustment that may increase the accuracy of formulas that describe the growth of publications in a subject field. It is named after mathematician Kenneth O. May (b. 1915).

In the first *sample reference*, May collects data on the number of publications in mathematics from 1868 through 1965. Prior to introducing the correction, May (1966, p. 1672) produces a formula that describes the growth of mathematical publications during those years:

$$n = 1400e^{0.025(t-1880)},$$

where:

n is the number of documents published in the year t;
e is the number 2.71828. . . .

For example,

$$\begin{aligned}
\text{if } t = 1868, \text{ then } n &= 1400*e^{0.025(1868-1880)} = 1400*e^{-0.3} \\
&= 1400*0.741 = 1037 \text{ documents;} \\
\text{if } t = 1900, \text{ then } n &= 1400*e^{0.025(1900-1880)} = 1400*e^{0.5} \\
&= 1400*1.649 = 2309 \text{ documents;} \\
\text{if } t = 1965, \text{ then } n &= 1400*e^{0.025(1965-1880)} = 1400*e^{2.125} \\
&= 1400*8.373 = 11,722 \text{ documents.}
\end{aligned}$$

These results from the formula compare well with May's actual count of publications in those years.

What instigates the correction is that May is especially interested in creating a formula that describes the cumulative growth of the literature of mathematics. So, even though his data begin with 1868, May cannot ignore the mathematics documents published prior to 1868. He estimates that there are 41,000 mathematics publications that he would have counted if he had extended his survey before 1868. This is the correction, and it leads to the equation:

$$n = 56,000e^{0.025(t-1880)},$$

where:

t and e are the same as above, but n now stands for the cumulative number of documents published by the end of year t (May, 1966, p. 1672).

For example,

$$\begin{aligned}
\text{if } t = 1867, \text{ then } n &= 56000*e^{0.025(1867-1880)} = 56000*e^{-0.325} \\
&= 56000*0.723 = 40,488 \text{ documents;} \\
\text{if } t = 1965, \text{ then } n &= 56000*e^{0.025(1965-1880)} = 56000*e^{2.125} \\
&= 56000*8.373 = 468,888 \text{ documents.}
\end{aligned}$$

The last result is somewhat close to May's count of about 419,000 documents published through the end of 1965.

In the second *sample reference*, Efthimiadis (1990) applies May's correction to an analysis of the growth of the literature on library online public access catalogs during 1970-1985. Interesting problems arise because there may well be no literature on this topic prior to 1970.

mean citation age. An infrequently used measure of synchronous obsolescence (**obsolescence, synchronous**). Median citation age is more commonly used.

Compare with **citation age; currency; half life; half life, cited; half life, citing; immediacy index; Price's index; recency score**.

In the *sample reference*, Wallace (1986) compares mean citation ages and median citation ages of the desalination literature.

mean response time. A measure of what some would call citation speed: the speed with which articles in a journal are used and cited. It is a type of time lag (**time lag, citation**).

Mean response time for a journal during a certain period is the average response time for all the articles published by the journal during that period. (The response time of any article is the number of months or years between the publication of the article and the date of the first time it is cited.)

In the *sample reference*, Schubert and Glanzel (1986) introduce the mean response time and calculate it for 109 physics journals.

For example, suppose one is calculating the mean response time of the articles published in a certain journal during 1991. Look for citations to each of these articles in a predetermined group of journals in the subject field being analyzed. Then place a reasonable limit on the response time. The writers in the *sample reference* suggest five years for physics journals. This requires looking for citations in the 1991-95 issues of the journals in the subject area. Keep in mind that it is necessary only to record the date of the first citation received by each of the articles.

Suppose there are 50 articles published in 1991 in the journal being tested and that there are citations in 1991-95 as follows:

2 of the 50 articles receive their first citation in 1991;

5 of the 50 articles receive their first citation in 1992;

10 of the 50 articles receive their first citation in 1993;
6 of the 50 articles receive their first citation in 1994;
3 of the 50 articles receive their first citation in 1995;
24 of the 50 articles receive no citations during 1991-95.

Then, Schubert and Glanzel (1986, p. 125) give the following formula for calculating the mean response time for the journal:

$$MRT = -\ln (f_0 + e^{-1}f_1 + e^{-2}f_2 + e^{-3}f_3 + e^{-4}f_4)$$

where:

MRT is the mean response time;
ln is the natural logarithm;
f_0 is the fraction of the articles receiving their first citation during the year of publication of the articles (1991 in the example above);
f_1 is the fraction of the articles receiving their first citation during the 1st year after publication (1992);
f_2 is the fraction of the articles receiving their first citation during the 2nd year after publication (1993);
f_3 and f_4 are the respective fractions for 1994 and 1995;
e is the number 2.71828. . . .

So, in this example:

MRT =
$$-\ln (2/50 + e^{-1}5/50 + e^{-2}10/50 + e^{-3}6/50 + e^{-4}3/50)$$
$$= -\ln (.04 + .37*.10 + .14*.20 + .05*.12 + .02*.06)$$
$$= -\ln (.1122) = 2.19 \text{ years}$$

By using logarithms and the number e, the formula calculates an average response time even though the response time for some of the articles (24 in this example) is, in a sense, infinite.

Setting the limit of response to something other than 5 years would correspondingly change the formula. Therefore, for a 7-year limit, the formula would be:

MRT =
$$-\ln (f_0 + e^{-1}f_1 + e^{-2}f_2 + e^{-3}f_3 + e^{-4}f_4 + e^{-5}f_5 + e^{-6}f_6)$$

median citation age. A measure of synchronous obsolescence (**obsolescence, synchronous**). It is obtained by subtracting the median publication year of the references listed in a group of source documents from the publication year of the source documents.

For example, consider a group of source documents published in 1993. Let the following years be the publication dates of the items in their lists of references: 1990, 1990, 1990, 1989, 1989, 1989, 1988, 1988, 1987, 1987, 1987, 1986, 1986, <u>1986</u>, 1986, 1984, 1983, 1983, 1981, 1978, 1977, 1973, 1972, 1970, 1966, 1965, 1960. The underlined 1986 is the median or middle year of the 27 dates. Then, 1993 minus 1986 equals seven. So, the median citation age in this analysis is seven years. The exact value of the median year (and, hence, the median citation age) may differ depending on the statistical technique used to calculate a median.

The median citation age of the references in a single source document is sometimes called the **recency score**.

Infrequently a mean citation age is calculated. The mean of the reference years above is about 1982. So, the mean citation age of the source documents is 1993 minus 1982, which is eleven years.

Compare with **citation age**; **currency**; **half life**; **half life, cited**; **half life, citing**; **immediacy index**; **Price's index**; **recency score**.

In the *sample reference*, Stinson and Lancaster (1987) calculate median citation ages for the genetics literature.

minimum Bradford nucleus. *See* **Bradford nucleus, minimum**.

mobility. A measure of communication at a professional conference.

In the *sample reference*, Chatelin and Arvanitis (1992) define mobility as the ratio of the number of papers delivered at conferences in a given subject field to the number of publications in that field.

model. An ideal description of an activity. In bibliometrics a model is usually expressed as a mathematical formula, although some models can be expressed graphically or verbally.

BASIC INFORMATION

Two examples of activities that can be modelled are: (1) the relation between number of articles published in a field and the number of journals in which they are located; and (2) the relation between the time of day or year and the number of books borrowed from a library.

Modelers and their critics test the models to see how well they describe the given activity. For example, a model of Bradford's law may be tested in various subject fields to see if the model's formula accurately describes the way articles on a given topic are scattered among various journals. A model of library circulation may be tested by seeing how well it predicts circulation activity in libraries.

Some may use model synonymously with "version" or "form." So, it may be said that there are various models or versions or forms of each of the major bibliometric laws.

Some may use model synonymously with the terms: **cumulative distribution function, frequency distribution, frequency distribution function, probability distribution, mathematical function** or simply **distribution** or **function**. In this case, model refers to a theoretical expression of a bibliometric law.

EXAMPLES OF MODELS

In the first *sample reference*, Lotka (1926) describes publication patterns of physics and chemistry documents (**Lotka's law**). In more recent years, bibliometricians have developed models to test how well the law applies to various groups of documents.

In the second *sample reference*, Nicholls (1989) notes the steps in establishing and testing a model. For example, one of the steps in testing a model for Lotka's law is to estimate the parameters of the model. Here is a version of Lotka's law, with b and k as the parameters.

$$g(x) = kx^{-b}$$

where:

$g(x)$ is the probability than an author produces x publications;
b and k are parameters that depend on the field being tested.

Nicholls examines how well this formula fits actual data for values of b between 1.5 and 3.0.

The third *sample reference* tests the applicability of probability distributions, such as the Gaussian-Poisson distribution, as models of the patterns of references found at the end of a group of research papers (Sichel, 1992).

In the fourth *sample reference*, Bookstein (1990) notes two competing models for the occurrence of words in a text. The first model is associated with Zipf's law, the second with Mandelbrot's law:

First model: Second model:

$r * y = A$ $y = A/[(1+Br)^a]$

where:

y is the number of times a word occurs in the text;

r is the rank of the word, with rank=1 being the highest ranked word;

A, B, and a are parameters that depend on the text being analyzed.

motivation, citation. *See* **citation type**.

multiple authorship. *See* **authorship, multiple**.

multisynchronous obsolescence. *See* **obsolescence, multisynchronous**.

mutual citations. *See* **citations, mutual**.

N

negative binomial distribution. One of the many probability distributions used in bibliometrics. It has the following form:

$$P(Y = k) = \frac{(k-1)!}{(k-r)!(r-1)!} * p^r q^{k-r}, \text{ for } k >= r$$

where:

P(Y = k) is the probability that it will take k trials to obtain r successes;
p is the probability of success;
q = 1 - p;
! is the factorial operation.
(James, 1976, p. 32)

In the *sample reference*, Sichel (1992) uses this and other distributions to test models of the number of references at the end of scientific papers.

noncitation. *See* **citation, internal; uncitedness.**

normal count. *See* **complete count.**

normative theory of citing. *See* **citing, normative theory of.**

nuclear zone. *See* **Bradford nucleus.**

nucleus. *See* **Bradford nucleus.**

O

obsolescence. The decrease in use of a document or group of documents as the documents become older. Also called **ageing, aging, decay**.

When applied to a whole subject field, obsolescence is also known as the aging/ageing or decay of the literature of that field. In a library, circulation statistics may be a measure of obsolescence.

Bibliometricians often use citation data to analyze obsolescence. If a document is cited less and less frequently, it is obsolescing. Citation based measures of obsolescence include median citation age and half life.

Two basic types of obsolescence are synchronous and diachronous (**obsolescence, synchronous; obsolescence, diachronous**). Because bibliometricians often study the former, obsolescence is sometimes considered synonymous with synchronous obsolescence.

If a group of documents receives few citations after only a few years in existence, the documents are said to have high obsolescence, to obsolesce quickly, or to age quickly. Documents that continue to get cited year after year are said to have low obsolescence, to obsolesce slowly, or age slowly.

In the first *sample reference*, Price (1965) uses the metaphors of life and death for the absence and presence of obsolescence. Death of a paper is considered synonymous with never being cited again.

In the second *sample reference*, Heisey (1988) finds that in documents dealing with the Dead Sea Scrolls, critical papers obsolesce more slowly than archaeological papers.

In the third *sample reference*, Wallace (1987) describes obsolescence studies of library collections.

obsolescence, diachronous. A type of obsolescence that measures the aging of a group of documents through an examination of the publication dates of citations that the documents receive. Half life is the measure of diachronous obsolescence. Other types of obsolescence are: **obsolescence, diasynchronous; obsolescence, multi-**

synchronous; and **obsolescence, synchronous**. As an example of diachronous obsolescence, consider a group of source documents published in 1974. Let the following years be the publication dates of the documents that cite the source documents:

1975 (9 citations)	1983 (7)
1976 (6)	1984 (5)
1977 (7)	1985 (7)
1978 (6)	1986 (2)
1979 (7)	1987 (5)
1980 (7)	1988 (2)
1981 (7)	1989 (2)
1982 (3)	1990 (1)

The median or middle year of the 83 dates is 1980. Then, 1980 minus 1974 equals six years. So, the half life in this analysis is six years. The exact value of the median year (and, hence, the half life) may differ depending on the statistical technique used to calculate a median.

In the *sample reference*, Stinson and Lancaster (1987) compare synchronous and diachronous analyses of documents in genetics.

obsolescence, diasynchronous. A type of synchronous obsolescence (**obsolescence, synchronous**) that measures the aging of a group of documents while taking into account the growth of the subject area being analyzed.

Also called multisynchronous obsolescence (**obsolescence, multisynchronous**).

Other types of obsolescence are: **obsolescence, diachronous** and **obsolescence, synchronous**.

In the *sample reference*, Heisey (1988) introduces the reference density ratio to account for the growth of the literature of the Dead Sea Scrolls. Because this literature is well defined, it is possible to identify the entire population of potential citing and cited documents (cited document and citing document).

For example, in the same *sample reference*, Heisey creates a random sample of 300 documents from a population of 7,489 documents and examines the references (or, synonymously, the citations) listed in the 300 sampled documents. There are citations between 0 and 35 years old, including:

353 references that are 1 year old;
  that is, each reference is a citation to a document published 1
  year prior to the publication of the citing document;
186 references that are 10 years old;
  that is, each reference is a citation to a document published 10
  years prior to the publication of the citing document;
60 references that are 20 years old.

The writer reports that there are:

7,435 citable documents and 7,461 potentially citing documents
  that have attained an age of at least 1 year;
6,207 citable documents and 4,877 potentially citing documents
  that have attained an age of at least 10 years;
4,942 citable documents and 2,290 potentially citing documents
  that have attained an age of at least 20 years.

The writer combines the two sets of data above to calculate the reference density ratio for each age:

for documents of age 1 year, reference density ratio is:
  $353/7435/7461 = 0.0000063$;
for documents of age 10 years, reference density ratio is:
  $186/6207/4877 = 0.0000061$;
for documents of age 20 years, reference density ratio is:
  $60/4942/2290 = 0.0000053$.
(Heisey, 1988, p. 292)

The closeness of the three results (as well as data for all the remaining ages) led Heisey (1988) to note that reference density ratios "show no clear decline at all" in use of the older literature (p. 293).

obsolescence, multisynchronous. A type of synchronous obsolescence that measures the aging of a group of documents that are published over a range of years. It is the range of years that elicits the prefix "multi." The alternative to doing a multisynchronous analysis is to study the synchronous obsolescence (**obsolescence, synchronous**) of documents all published in the same year. In both alternatives, median citation age is how one usually expresses the obsolescence.

Also called diasynchronous obsolescence (**obsolescence, diasynchronous**). Compare with **obsolescence, diachronous**.

Consider an example of calculating the median citation age in multisynchronous obsolescence. There are two source documents, one published in 1992 and one published in 1993. In their respective bibliographies, they list documents that have the publications dates and ages indicated below.

Publication Dates of the Source Documents	Publication Dates (and Ages) of the References
1992	1990 (2 years); 1990 (2 years); 1989 (3 years); 1989 (3 years); 1988 (4 years); 1988 (4 years); 1987 (5 years); 1987 (5 years); 1986 (6 years); 1984 (8 years); 1983 (9 years); 1983 (9 years); 1981 (11 years); 1970 (22 years); 1965 (27 years).
1993	1990 (3 years); 1989 (4 years); 1987 (6 years); 1986 (7 years); 1986 (7 years); 1986 (7 years); 1978 (15 years); 1977 (16 years); 1973 (20 years); 1972 (21 years); 1966 (27 years); 1960 (33 years).

A list of the ages of all 27 references, from youngest to oldest, is: 2, 2, 3, 3, 3, 4, 4, 4, 5, 5, 6, 6, 7, 7, 7, 8, 9, 9, 11, 15, 16, 20, 21, 22, 27, 27, 33. The underlined 7 is the median or middle age of the 27 ages. So, the median citation age of the references is seven years. The exact value of the median age (and hence, the median citation age) may differ depending on the statistical technique used to calculate a median.

In the *sample reference,* Wallace (1986) analyzes the obsolescence of desalination documents published in the 1970s.

obsolescence, synchronous. A type of obsolescence that measures the aging of a group of documents by examining the publication dates of the references in those documents. Median citation age is the usual measure of synchronous obsolescence.

For example, consider a group of documents published in 1993. Let the following years be the publication dates of the items in their lists of references: 1990, 1990, 1990, 1989, 1989, 1989, 1988, 1988, 1987, 1987, 1987, 1986, 1986, 1986, 1986, 1984, 1983, 1983, 1981, 1978, 1977, 1973, 1972, 1970, 1966, 1965, 1960. The underlined 1986 is the median or middle year of the 27 dates. Then, 1993 minus 1986 equals seven. So, the median citation age of the references is seven years. The exact value of the median year (and, hence, the median citation age) may differ depending on the statistical technique used to calculate a median.

Because bibliometricians often do synchronous analyses, synchronous obsolescence is sometimes called simply: obsolescence. Compare with **obsolescence, diachronous**; **obsolescence, diasynchronous**; and **obsolescence, multisynchronous**.

In the *sample reference*, Stinson and Lancaster (1987) compare synchronous and diachronous analyses of documents in genetics.

Ortega hypothesis. The claim that research by average scientists is important to the advancement of science.

In the first *sample reference*, Cole and Cole (1972) may be the first to use this term. They attribute this concept to, among others, philosopher Jose Ortega y Gasset (1883-1955).

In the second *sample reference*, Ortega y Gasset (1957) discusses the "barbarism of 'specialisation'" in the physical and biological sciences. He says:

> What happens is that, enclosed within the narrow limits of his visual field, he [the specialized scientist] does actually succeed in discovering new facts and advancing the progress of the science which he hardly knows, and incidentally the encyclopedia of thought of which he is conscientiously ignorant. How has such a thing been possible, how is it still possible? For it is necessary to insist upon this extraordinary but undeniable fact: experimental science has progressed thanks in great part to the work of men astoundingly mediocre, and even less than mediocre. That is to say, modern science, the root and symbol of our actual civilisation, finds a place for the intellectually commonplace man and allows him to work therein with success. (pp. 110-111)

In the third *sample reference*, Kretschmer and Muller (1990) mention the Ortega hypothesis as they test the relationship between publication rate of scientists and how well they are connected to their field (how eminent they are), as measured by such factors as co-authorship.

output. *See* **research performance**.

outside citation. *See* **citation, outside**.

overlap. *See* **coverage overlap**.

P

pagination range. Characterization of a document by the number of pages it contains.

In the first *sample reference*, Kazlauskas, DeYoe, and Smith (1989) find that most of the periodical issues they examine fall into either the 50-100 page or 100-150 page range.

In the second *sample reference*, Fisher (1991) demonstrates the growth of the endocrinology literature by showing increases in the number of journal pages in the field between 1917 and 1990.

parameter. A variable that changes from case to case in a mathematical expression.

For example, in the following expression of Lotka's law, n and c are the parameters.

$$x^n y = c$$

where:

y is the portion of authors making x contributions each;
n and c are parameters that depend on the field being analyzed.

In the first *sample reference*, Lotka (1926) examines authorship of chemistry publications. They produce values of $n = 1.888$ and $c = 0.5669$.

In the second *sample reference*, Pao (1986) reviews 48 sets of authorship data from various subject fields. When expressed using Lotka's law, these 48 cases produce values of n between 1.7828 and 3.7747 and values of c between 0.5239 and 0.9094.

Pareto's law. A concept borrowed from economics. It is named for sociologist and economist Vilfredo Pareto (1848-1923).

According to the first *sample reference*, Pareto's law analyzes the richest members of a community:

$$r = \frac{A}{y^a}$$

where:

r is the number of individuals who earn more than y dollars annually;

A and a are parameters that depend on the community being analyzed.

Bookstein (1990) notes that Pareto's law and Zipf's law are versions of each other, if the r in the above formula is considered a rank.

In the second *sample reference*, Rousseau (1990b) expresses Pareto's law in terms closer to bibliometrics than to economics:

$$y(r) = \frac{K}{r^v}$$

y(r) is the number of items (or articles) produced by a source (or a journal) ranked at place r among all the sources (or journals) analyzed;

K and v are parameters that depend on the subject field being analyzed.

partition. *See* **Bradford partition.**

patent analysis. The counting of patents and citations to patents produced by one or more countries or organizations over a specified period of time. Such analyses may demonstrate the technological and economic importance of the given countries or organizations. Therefore, patent analysis can be a science indicator for a country or organization.

In the *sample reference*, Narin (1991) compares the number of patents to the gross domestic product for members of the European Communities.

peer interactive communication. A type of acknowledgement that authors place in their articles. The peer interactive communication gives thanks to colleagues for having provided advice, criticisms, inspiration, or suggestions.

In the first *sample reference*, Cronin, McKenzie, and Stiffler (1992) analyze this and other types of acknowledgement in twenty years of four library and information science journals.

The second *sample reference* develops the categorization of acknowledgements upon which the authors in the first *sample reference* base part of their analysis (McCain, 1991a).

peer review. Evaluation of one's work by a colleague. In bibliometrics and scholarly communication, this usually refers to the evaluation of a manuscript submitted to a journal for possible publication. Also called **refereeing**.

In the first *sample reference*, Biggs (1990) gives a history of peer review and then covers such issues as the blindness controversy, the impact of peer review on intellectual freedom, and the conservativeness of the process.

In the second *sample reference*, Gidez (1991) surveys members of the Federation of American Societies for Experimental Biology (FASEB) on their activities and perceptions as authors and peer reviewers for the *FASEB Journal*.

performance, research. *See* **research performance.**

peripheral journal. A journal that (1) devotes only a small part of its content to the subject area being analyzed, and/or (2) in some way is relatively unimportant in its subject area.

The first meaning is more quantitative than qualitative. An example is a general education journal that is peripheral to the subject area of reading because it carries articles from many areas of education, only a few of which deal with reading. A peripheral journal can be considered the opposite of a core journal, though core journal is a more formal term because of its association with Bradford's law and the Bradford nucleus or core.

The second meaning is more qualitative than quantitative. An example is a reading journal that is peripheral in its own field–reading–because it is not well known, espouses radical ideas, is available in a very small geographic area or for some other reason. An analysis, such as a citation analysis, may be a way to determine how peripheral a journal is.

In the *sample reference* Stolte-Heiskanen (1986) discusses indicators, like citations, as a way to identify the center and periphery of a field. The emphasis here is on the qualitative meaning of peripheral and on geographic areas.

Poisson distribution. One of the many probability distributions used in bibliometrics. It is named for mathematician Simeon Denis Poisson (1781-1840). One form of it is:

$$P_n(k) = \frac{e^{-a}a^k}{k!}$$

where:

> $P_n(k)$ is the probability of obtaining k successes in n trials in a situation in which successes rarely occur and there are many trials;
> e is the number 2.71828 . . . . ;
> ! is the factorial operation;
> a equals n multiplied by the probability of a success.
> (James, 1976, p. 293)

In the *sample reference*, Ajiferuke (1991) examines various distributions, including some Poisson-like distributions, as models of authorship patterns in 94 collections of documents.

popularity factor. A measure of the popularity or impact of a journal. The popularity factor of journal A during a certain period is the number of journals that cite articles published in journal A divided by the number of journals that journal A's own articles cite.

For example, during 1994-95, journal A is cited by 15 journals. During that same time, the articles in journal A cite articles in 45 journals. So, the popularity factor for journal A is 15/45 = 0.33.

Also called **journal popularity factor**. Compare with **impact factor**. Popularity factor is one of the components of the consumption factor of a journal.

In the *sample reference*, Yanovksy (1991) introduces the popularity factor and shows how it can be used to calculate a journal's consumption factor.

popularization. A retelling of a technical matter so that the average person can understand. The term usually refers to the popularization of scientific and technical material but can apply to any subject matter. The original information is often in the form of a research publication or announcement. The popularization can be a magazine article, a book, or a news report.

Compare with **bridge paper**, which is usually meant for someone who knows the subject field well but is more of an applier than a theoretician or researcher.

An article in *Scientific American* that explains the laws of bibliometrics to the intelligent layperson would be a popularization. An article in *Library Journal* or *American Libraries* that helps librarians apply bibliometric research to evaluation of library services would be a bridge paper.

In the *sample reference*, Hilgartner (1990) does a case study of various popularizations of a single piece of research. The analysis shows how the popularizations differ from the original in their descriptions of the authors and content of the research.

Pratt's measure. A measure of how concentrated or spread out items (like journal articles) are when they are divided into categories. The nature of the categories is decided by each person who uses this measure. Pratt's measure is named for bibliometrician Allan D. Pratt (b. 1933).

For example, consider all the articles that have been written by three bibliometricians, A, B, and C. They have written 150 articles each. Categorize the articles by the type of bibliometrics they describe. Write out the categories and rank the categories by the numbers of articles they contain.

Bibliometrician A has written:
   80 articles on citation analysis (rank of 1);
   35 articles on Bradford's law (rank of 2);
   20 articles on Lotka's law (rank of 3);
   12 articles on research performance (rank of 4);
   3 articles on Pratt's measure (rank of 5).

Bibliometrician B has written:
   145 articles on citation analysis (rank of 1);
   5 articles on Pratt's measure (rank of 2).

Bibliometrician C has written:
   30 articles on citation analysis (rank of 1);
   30 articles on Bradford's law (rank of 2);
   30 articles on Lotka's law (rank of 3);

30 articles on research performance (rank of 4);
30 articles on Pratt's measure (rank of 5).

Without doing any calculations, one can see that bibliometrician B's articles are very concentrated in citation analysis; bibliometrician A's articles are somewhat concentrated in that same area; and bibliometrician C's articles are spread out evenly among all five categories. Pratt's measure formalizes this finding.

In the first *sample reference*, Pratt (1977) gives the measure as:

$$C = \frac{2\ [((n\ +\ 1)/2) - q]}{n - 1}$$

where:

C is Pratt's measure of concentration;
n is the number of categories;
q is the sum of ranks times frequencies for a given category, divided by the number of items in all the categories.

So, for bibliometrician A, n = 5 and:

$$q = (80*1 + 35*2 + 20*3 + 12*4 + 3*5)/150 = 1.82$$

and

$$C = \frac{2\ [((5\ +\ 1)/2) - 1.82]}{5 - 1} = \frac{2.36}{4} = 0.59$$

Because Pratt's measure has a maximum of 1.00 and a minimum of 0.00, bibliometrician A's score of 0.59 may be called moderately concentrated. It turns out that bibliometrician B's score is 0.94 (very concentrated), and bibliometrician C's score is 0 (very non-concentrated or scattered).

In the second *sample reference*, Egghe and Rousseau (1991, p. 479) note that Pratt's measure is "[t]he most used measure of concentration in informetrics. . . ."

Compare with **concentration, informetrics**.

Price's index. A measure of the recency of the citations in a document, journal, or an entire subject field. It is the ratio of the number of citations that are no more than five years old to the total number of citations. It is infrequently known as Price's immediacy index, but should not be confused with the measure known simply as the immediacy index.

Compare with **currency, half life, median citation age, recency score**.

In the first *sample reference*, Price (1970) introduces it as Price's index (p. 10).

In the second *sample reference* Braam, Moed, and van Raan (1991a) suggest Price's index as a means to identify a research front.

Price's law. A rule describing the number of prolific authors in a subject field. In a given field during a given period of time, the number of prolific authors is equal to approximately the square root of the total number of authors in the field. In particular, the prolific authors account for about half the publications in the field. It is named for Derek J. de Solla Price (1922- 1983). Also called **Price's square root law**.

For example, assume that an analysis of a subject field finds 550 authors who produce a total of 1700 publications. The square root of 550 authors is about 23 authors. Half of 1700 publications is 850 publications. So, Price's law says that approximately 23 prolific authors should have produced about 850 of the publications.

In the first *sample reference*, Price (1963) derives the law after discussing the ideas of Francis Galton (on elitism) and Alfred Lotka (on authorship in chemistry and physics). Price says:

> If one computes the total production of those who write n papers, it emerges that the large number of low producers account for about as much of the total as the small number of large producers; in a simple schematic case, symmetry may be shown to a point corresponding to the square root of the total number of men, or the score of the highest producer. (p. 46)

In the second *sample reference*, Nicholls (1988, p. 469) describes the relationship between Price's law and Lotka's law. The writer also notes that Price's law has its roots in Rousseau's law, which "had long been known in the social sciences. . . ."

Price's square root law. See Price's law.

primary author. *See* **author, primary.**

primary count. *See* **straight count.**

primary literature. *See* **literature, primary.**

principle of least effort. The idea that organisms, in many of their activities, seek the most efficient path or action. This principle may be a pervasive aspect of human life.

In the first *sample reference*, Zipf (1949) says: "The Principle of Least Effort [is] the primary principle that governs our entire individual and collective behavior of all sorts, including the behavior of our language and preconceptions" (p. viii).

Zipf's thoughts about the principle are linked to his work on the use of words in human speech and text. His analysis of word frequencies have resulted in Zipf's law.

probability distribution. *See* **distribution; model.**

probability distribution function. *See* **distribution.**

productivity, research. *See* **research performance.**

productivity, scientific. *See* **scientific productivity.**

publication count. The number of documents published by an author, journal, organization, or other source in a given period of time, perhaps limited to a given subject field or geographic area.

Complications can arise in counting publications if documents have multiple authors (**authorship, multiple**). In such cases, there are at least three ways to count authorship: **adjusted count, complete count,** and **straight count.**

publication potential. The number of authors or publications that a country, organization, or other group could produce in a given subject area if all individual experts in that field contributed. The most crucial aspect of this measure is the estimation of how many experts there are in a given field who do not publish.

In the *sample reference*, Schubert and Braun (1992) estimate the publication potential in science for 45 developing countries.

Q

quotation. *See* **referenced quotation.**

R

readability index. A measure of how easy or difficult a text is to read. Such an index may depend on such factors as the length and complexity of sentences. An examination of readability can be a first step in doing a content analysis.

Typical readability indexes are the **Dale-Chall readability formula; Danielson and Bryan readability index; Flesch readability ease score; FOG readability index**.

In the *sample reference* Shaw (1989) uses a software package to calculate the readability of online search user manuals.

recency score. The median age of the references listed in the bibliography of a document. It is equivalent to the median citation age of the references.

Compare with **currency, half life, immediacy index, Price's index**.

In the *sample reference*, Kidd (1990) uses the recency score to calculate a hot topic index for a document.

receptivity. The tendency of a document or author to cite another document or author. The citing item is said to have receptivity for the cited item. The cited document or author is said to have influence over the citing item.

In the *sample reference*, Everett and Pecotich (1991) examine a model of citations between journals based on receptivity and influence.

reconstruction. The compilation of a list of publications produced by an organization or other group of people for which there is no definitive list of the members of the group. Also called **bibliometric reconstruction**.

In the *sample reference*, Nederhof and Noyons (1992) use this procedure to help them gather citation data for university departments. They compile the publication lists by retrieving address data from *Arts & Humanities Citation Index*® and *Social Sciences Citation Index*®.

refereeing. *See* **peer review**.

reference. A publication mentioned in a document, usually in the document's footnotes, endnotes, bibliography, or list of references.

Sometimes reference is a synonym for citation. However, to see how they can be distinguished, consider the example of document A being listed among the footnotes in document B. Then, one can say that:

> document B gives document A as a reference;
> document B refers to document A;
> document B cites document A;

and that:

> document A receives a citation from document B;
> document A receives a reference from document B;
> document A is cited by document B.

reference density (a measure of references per words in a document). See **density ratio**.

reference density (the fraction of citable documents that are cited). See **density, citation**.

reference density ratio (a measure of obsolescence). See **obsolescence, diasynchronous**.

referenced quotation. The text that one book or article quotes verbatim from another. Enough bibliographic data is given so that the reader can find the original quote. Also called **quotation**.

In the *sample reference*, Kilgour and Feder (1992) analyze the number and size of referenced quotations in books. They note that such analyses may suggest ways to improve the indexing and searching of books.

relative standing. *See* **standing**.

research front. A subject field characterized by active research. It is well defined in the sense that there is a tendency for documents in the front to cite other documents in the front rather than documents outside the front.

To some, front suggests that the field may well be a new area of interest within an established field. This need not be.

Bibliometricians may describe the front by measuring the cocitation strengths between documents in the field and creating cocitation cluster maps.

In the first *sample reference*, Braam, Moed, and van Raan (1991a) do a citation analysis of biochemical research. They note that measures for identifying research fronts include: cocitation strength, immediacy index, and Price's index.

In the second *sample reference*, Garfield (1986a) describes how research fronts are identified for *Science Citation Index®*.

research output. *See* **research performance**.

research performance. A measure of the quantity or importance of research done by an individual, group, or even a country. Also called **output, research output, research productivity**.

One quantitative measure of research performance is the number of articles, books, and conference papers a person or group produces in a given period. Another measure of importance is the number of citations received by the person's or group's publications.

In the first *sample reference*, Garland (1991) examines the types of publications produced by library and information science faculty.

In the second *sample reference*, Kendrick (1991) reports the number and type of publications produced by business librarians with and without university faculty rank.

In the third *sample reference*, Nederhof and Noyons (1992) use citations as a way to compare the research performance of academic departments.

research productivity. *See* **research performance**.

response time. A measure of what some would call citation speed, in this case the speed with which a document is used and cited. It is a type of time lag (**time lag, citation**). Response time is the number of months or years between the publication of a document and the first time it is cited.

For example, if an article is published in the April, 1994 issue of a journal and is first cited by an article that appears in the September, 1996 issue of the same or some other journal, then the mean response time for the original article is:

September, 1996 minus April, 1994 = 2 years, 5 months;
                                                              = 29 months;
                                                              = 2.42 years.

In the *sample reference*, Schubert and Glanzel (1986) apply this measure to many articles and then calculate a mean response time for 109 physics journals.

Rich, Barnaby. *See* **Barnaby Rich effect.**

Rousseau's law. The idea that the size of the elite within a population is about equal to the square root of the population. The law is named for philosopher Jean Jacques Rousseau (1712-1778).

Rousseau's law is one of the sources for Price's law of authorship, which in turn also draws ideas from Lotka's law of authorship.

The sample references below suggest that the naming of the law may be more of an attribution of an idea rather than a claim that Rousseau discussed square roots.

In the first *sample reference*, Nicholls (1988) says that Rousseau's law "had long been known in the social sciences. . ." (p. 469).

In the second *sample reference*, Rescher (1978) extends the law beyond elite people to important results:

> There is good reason to think that–in virtually any context where a significant concept of importance is operative–the volume of really "important" production stands as the square root of the total production. . . . This is in fact a rather well-known formula in the study of elites, reflecting the principle that the elite of a group stand as the square root of its size. Such a relationship was initially mooted by Jean Jacques Rousseau. . . . (p. 97)

In the third *sample reference*, Zipf (1949) suggests the source of the law: "This statement that is so frequently imputed to J. J. Rousseau seems to evade specific reference although its sense is apparent in his *Contrat Social*" (p. 560).

The fourth *sample reference* is an English translation of Rousseau's own work. One of perhaps many places where he discusses the concept of elitism is in "A Discourse on the Origin of Inequality":

> In a word, I could prove that, if we have a few rich and powerful men on the pinnacle of fortune and grandeur, while the crowd grovels in want and obscurity, it is because the former prize what they enjoy only in so far as others are destitute of it. . . . (Rousseau, 1913, pp. 233-234)

S

sacred spark theory. An explanation for why scholars do research and publish papers. The sacred spark theory says they do it because they want to, because they enjoy it, because they get internal satisfaction from doing research. Although the sacred spark is used to explain at least some research performance in the life and physical sciences, it should be applicable to any field of study.

In the first *sample reference*, Cole and Cole (1973) may be the originators of the term. They contrast two hypotheses of research performance:

> Our hypothesis [is] that a reward system which rewards quality of output produces a high correlation between quantity and quality. . . . Simplified, it states that scientists who are rewarded are productive, and scientists who are not rewarded become less productive. An alternative explanation of the data, one held by many scientists and historians of science, might be called the "sacred spark" theory. Adherents of this theory would argue that scientists do science not because they are rewarded but because they have an inner compulsion to do so. (pp. 114-115)

In the second *sample reference*, Schwartz (1991) mentions the sacred spark during a discussion of research performance in library science.

scatter(ing). The spread of items among many different sources. This often refers to Bradford's law, which suggests that in a comprehensive collection of articles on a given topic covering some time period, there will be many journals (sources) that each publish only a few articles (items) on the topic. Compare with **core and scatter**.

In the *sample reference*, Czerwon, 1990 (p. 16) examines articles on Monte Carlo methods in lattice field theory. Eight journals account for about 90 percent of the articles, but the other 10 percent of the articles (48 articles) are scattered among 27 journals.

scholarliness. A characterization of how well researched a document is. Scholarliness can be quantified as the number of citations that the document lists in its footnotes or list of references. This quantification may be accompanied by an analysis of the reasons why the author uses the citations (**citation type**).

In the first *sample reference*, Price (1970) may be the first to suggest counting citations as a measure of scholarliness. He says: "[P]erhaps it is reasonable to identify the amount of . . . footnotage and referencing with our intuitive idea of 'scholarliness'" (p. 7).

In the second *sample reference*, Peritz (1983) compares scholarliness (number of citations listed in a bibliography) and impact (number of citations received by a document) for publications in sociology.

In the third *sample reference*, Schrader and Beswick (1989) say that "[a]n indication of scholarliness . . . is the presence in written works of bibliographic citations or references to other works." However, they caution that a large number of citations does not necessarily make a document very scholarly (p. 10).

In the fourth *sample reference*, Lockett and Khawam (1990) define scholarliness of a journal as the "ratio of articles with references to the total number of articles published by that journal" (p. 284). They then compare the scholarliness of two library science journals.

scholarly communication. A field that studies how scholars, scientists, and other professionals communicate with each other. Matters for examination include formal and informal communication (**communication, formal; communication, informal**), the invisible college, and information seeking behavior.

A major link with bibliometrics is the use of citation analysis to evaluate how and if scholars communicate through their publications. Such analyses, especially when they examine cocitations, may help researchers identify groups of scholars who have common subject interests.

The first *sample reference* is a monograph of studies that link bibliometrics and scholarly communication. It is based on a special October, 1989 issue of *Communication Research* (Borgman, 1990).

The second *sample reference* is an editorial on how scholarly communication should work, and how libraries may be affected as the scholarly journal is transformed into an electronic service (Rogers and Hurt, 1990).

The third *sample reference* is a special issue of *Science & Technology Libraries* devoted to communication and information seeking behaviors of scientists and engineers (Steinke, 1991).

Science Citation Index®. A publication of the Institute for Scientific Information. In its citation index it indicates who cites whom, and so it is often a source of data for citation analysis in the life and physical sciences.

science, hard and soft. A characterization that distinguishes scholarly fields by such matters as how quantitative they are. The harder sciences are the more quantitative. The theories or laws of the harder sciences (laws of motion, for example) appear to be less open to debate than those of the softer sciences (laws of behavior, for example).

The distinction may be less and less appropriate as many fields become more and more quantified. Insofar as such distinctions exist, they may be of interest to those who study scholarly communication.

science indicator. A measure that provides information about activity in the life and physical sciences, often in a specific country or area of the world.

Examples of science indicators include the amount and type of: citations to and from scientific publications; academic degrees awarded; government funding; languages used in science publications; patents; and scientists employed. Some of these indicators are used to describe research performance and scientific productivity.

Also called **scientific indicator, scientometric indicator**. Compare with **bibliometric indicator**.

In the *sample reference*, Alestalo (1992) reports on science indicators in Finland, including: government expenditures for universities; number of scientists at universities; and proportion of laws devoted to the expansion of science.

science of science. The study of research patterns in the life and physical sciences. It can be used synonymously with **scientometrics**, which is the preferred term today.

In the *sample reference*, Zmaic, Maricic, and Simeon (1989, p. 713) use the science of science terminology during a report on a citation analysis of chemistry journals.

science-profession dyad. Two groups of individuals who work in similar or identical subject fields. One group works in the science of the field; these are the research scientists or theoreticians or academicians. The other group works in the field's profession; these are the practitioners or applied scientists. Compare with boundary-spanning communication (**communication, boundary-spanning**). Also called **dyad**.

Workers in scholarly communication can study the communication between the two groups as well as each group's use of the literature of the field (**literature, primary**; **literature, secondary**).

In the *sample reference*, Martin (1992) examines the science of ichthyology and the corresponding profession of fisheries biology.

science, sociology of. A field of study that deals with physical and life scientists and how their activities affect and are affected by their social relations with each other and with the time and place in which they live and work.

A sociologist of science may study: interactions among colleagues in a laboratory; the sociological reasons for the acceptance of some scientific ideas and the rejection of others; scientists' roles in controversy; the development of scientific knowledge; how change is accepted; and so on.

Some of this overlaps with scientometrics, especially when the study becomes quantitative or examines publications.

The first *sample reference* falls into this overlap. Kyvik (1990) analyzes the relationship between documents produced by a scientist and the scientist's gender and number of children.

The second *sample reference* is an editorial from a major journal in this field. Originally named *Science Studies* in 1971, it changed its name in 1975 to *Social Studies of Science*. The same editorial appeared in the first issues for 1971 and 1975. It suggests that social studies of science include the study of:

> the social characteristics of science and technology, the political and economic influences affecting scientific and technological development, and the impact of science and technology on the condition of modern society. (Edge and MacLeod, 1975, p. 3)

In the third *sample reference*, Barber (1990), a pioneer in the field, notes that "the sociology of science did not exist, nor was even conceived of as a specialty in sociology" until the 1960s (p. 28). Barber also notes that "[t]he only professional sociologist writing about science in the 1930s and 1940s was the then-young (only in his twenties and thirties) Robert K. Merton. . . ." (p. 26).

science, soft. *See* **science, hard and soft.**

scientific indicator. *See* **science indicator.**

scientific productivity. The amount of research produced by scientists. Compare with **research performance, science indicator.**
Scientific productivity in many fields (in and out of the life and physical sciences) is measured by such data as the number of publications produced by authors in the field and the number of citations received by those publications. Measures of productivity also include counts of the scientists in the field, often for an entire country or area of the world.
In the *sample reference*, Schubert and Telcs (1989) compare numbers of publications and scientists among the 50 states of the United States.

scientometric indicator. *See* **science indicator.**

scientometrics. The mathematical and statistical analysis of research patterns in the life and physical sciences. Some of scientometrics is simply bibliometrics applied to the sciences. However, scientometrics also analyzes the "structure and development" (a quote from a definition below); scholarly communication; information seeking behavior; and government policy as related to the sciences. Also called **science of science**.

According to the first *sample reference*:

> Of course, the term "naukometrija" or "Scientometrics" has been used in the U.S.S.R. (where it originated) and the rest of Eastern Europe for many years (the exact time is not known by me) but only introduced in the west by the foundation of the journal "Scientometrics" in September 1978. . . . (Egghe, 1988a, p. 180)

According to the second *sample reference*:

> [Scientometrics is] the quantitative mathematical study of science and technology. Scientometrics is not characterized by its focus on particular problem areas but by its methodology, that is to say the use of quantitative indicators of the structure and development of science in order to decide the basic regularities of their functioning and direction. The research area investigated in the scientometric tradition covers a very wide range of topics: the quantitative growth of science . . . ; the specialty substructure in science . . . ; the development of disciplines . . . ; the relationship of science and technology . . . ; the "half-life" of scientific contributions . . . ; the communication structure in science and in technology . . . ; the conditions and measurement of productivity and creativity of scientists . . . ; the relationship between scientific development and economic growth . . . ; the structure and development of scientific manpower . . . ; and the criteria for investment in science. . . .
> This term [scientometrics] has been coined by Derek de Solla Price, who initiated this field of research. . . . (Spiegel-Rosing, 1977, p. 18)

In the third *sample reference*, Price himself comments on some of this etymology. He is quoted from the enlarged, 1975 edition of a book originally published in 1961:

> The material covered in this chapter has probably undergone more development and change than any other. It rapidly

proved to have a life of its own, so that it grew first into a separate book (*Little Science, Big Science . . .*) and then touched off a continuing series of research papers exploring many different quantitative investigations based on the counting of journals, papers, authors, and citations. In no time at all there were bibliographies and conventions devoted to *bibliometrics* and *scientometrics*, and even a meeting of the invisible college or people studying invisible colleges. . . . [T]he term "science of science" achieved an almost explosive popularity. Unfortunately, though it came readily to the tongue and pleased those who desired objective investigations of the workings of science in society, the term rapidly became debased by being used in as many different ways as there were users, and by being taken as a promise to deliver goods that were by their very nature undeliverable. (Price, 1975, pp. 193-194)

The first chapter in Price's 1963 book, *Little Science, Big Science* is called "A Science of Science." The fourth *sample reference* quotes from the Preface:

My approach will be to deal statistically, in a not very mathematical fashion, with general problems of the shape and size of science and the ground rules governing growth and behavior of science-in-the-large. . . . [T]reating science as a measurable entity, I shall attempt to develop a calculus of scientific manpower, literature, talent, and expenditure on a national and on an international scale. (Price, 1963, p. viii)

According to the fifth *sample reference*, the coverage of the journal *Scientometrics* includes:

. . . results of research concerned with the quantitative features and characteristics of science. Emphasis is made on investigations in which the development and the mechanism of science are studied by means of (statistical) mathematical methods. (Elsevier Science Publishers, 1992)

secondary author. *See* **author, secondary.**

secondary literature. *See* **literature, secondary.**

self citation. Usually a citation for which an individual is an author of both the cited document and citing document. This term is sometimes used only for an individual who is either the sole author or primary author (**author, primary**) of the documents. Compare with hidden self citation (**self citation, hidden**), **autocitation**.

In the first *sample reference*, Tagliacozzo (1977) suggests that self citation sometimes refers to: (1) a journal, when both citing and cited documents are published in the same journal, or (2) an organization, when authors of the citing and cited documents are associated with that organization. In these two cases, it is not necessary for the citing and cited documents to have an author in common (pp. 251-252).

In the second *sample reference*, MacRoberts and MacRoberts (1989) find that self citations can present problems when doing a citation analysis.

self citation, hidden. A self citation that is hidden in the sense that the author who cites him/herself is not the first listed author of the citing document.

Therefore, a hidden self citation requires that: (1) the citing document has more than one author, and (2) an author other than the primary author (**author, primary**) of the citing document is also an author of the cited document. The cited document may have single or multiple authorship (**authorship, multiple**).

In the *sample reference*, Zmaic, Maricic, and Simeon (1989) distinguish between hidden self citations and self citations by primary authors of citing documents.

senior author. *See* **author, primary**.

senior count. *See* **straight count**.

similarity. A measure of how alike two documents or authors are. The measure may be based on such factors as citations, cocitations, or word profiles. There are many ways to calculate such similarities. Similarities are also used outside of bibliometrics, especially in the field of information retrieval.

In a citation analysis of a group of authors, documents, or journals, the similarity measure may examine how much alike documents are in citing each other. For example, assume that Exhibit 15 is a citation matrix that gives the number of citations among a group of journals.

Then, journal C cites journal B six times; journal B cites journals C six times also. So, in some sense journals B and C are very similar.

However, journals A and B are dissimilar in this sense because A cites B five times, while B cites A only two times. Precise measures of similarity may use the inverse of a calculation similar to measuring the distance between points in space. Then, being very dissimilar is equivalent to being very far apart; two journals that are far apart would have a low similarity value.

In the *sample reference*, Everett and Pecotich (1991) create a model of citations among journals. In this model, the influence of a cited journal on a citing journal is calculated as the product of the cited journal's importance times the similarity between the two journals.

size of a literature. *See* **growth.**

slope. A measure of the steepness and direction of a line or curve on a graph.

EXHIBIT 15.
A citation matrix that provides data
for measuring the similarity between journals

Citing Journals

		A	B	C
	A	2	2	0
Cited				
	B	5	0	6
Journals				
	C	4	6	1

The slope between any two points on a line or curve on a two dimensional graph is the ratio of the difference in the y-axis values to the difference in the x-axis values of the points. Slope is also known as rise over run or as delta-y over delta-x.

For example, look at the line in Exhibit 16. Two of the points on the line are (5,12) and (1,3). The slope between the two points is:

$$\frac{(12-3)}{(5-1)} = \frac{9}{4} = 2.25$$

Special types of slopes are in the next two entries: **slope, bibliograph**; **slope, Cole**.

slope, bibliograph. In an analysis of Bradford's law, this is the slope of the bibliograph, the graph of the cumulative number of

EXHIBIT 16.
A line that has a slope of 2.25.

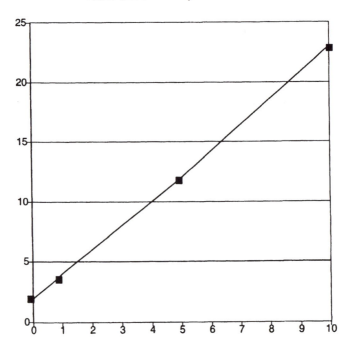

items (usually articles) on the vertical axis versus the logarithm of the ranks of the sources (usually journals) on the horizontal axis.

Some may prefer to plot the logarithm of the cumulative number of sources on the horizontal axis (rather than the logarithm of the ranks of the sources). Some may consider any Bradford curve to be a bibliograph.

The entry for bibliograph shows an example of a bibliograph in Exhibits 1a and 1b.

slope, Cole. In an analysis of Bradford's law, this is the slope of the curve that represents the cumulative fraction of items (usually articles) on the vertical axis versus the logarithm of the cumulative fraction of sources (usually journals) on the horizontal axis. It is named for bibliometrician P. F. Cole.

In the first *sample reference*, Cole (1962) suggests that this curve is usually close to a straight line and that the value of its slope is a way to characterize the field whose journals are being analyzed.

For example, Exhibit 17 contains data from the second *sample reference*. These are data that Bradford (1934) collected for articles in the field of applied geophysics.

The third line of data means, for example, that the three most productive journals cumulatively produced 235 articles. These three journals are 3/326 or .0092 of the total 326 journals. And their 235 articles are 235/1332 or .1764 of the total 1,332 articles.

To find the Cole slope of this data, first calculate the logarithm (common or natural) of the data in the column (c) of Exhibit 17 and place the results in column (e). This example uses common logarithms.

Next, make a graph having: the data from column (d) on the vertical axis, and the data from column (e) on the horizontal axis. Exhibit 18 shows this data on a graph.

Finally, the Cole slope is the slope of the straightest section of the curve in Exhibit 18. This occurs approximately between the points $(-1.37, 0.3814)$ and $(-0.48, 0.7995)$. The slope is:

$$\frac{0.7995 - 0.3814}{-0.48 - -1.37} = \frac{0.4181}{0.89} = 0.47$$

EXHIBIT 17.
Data for the graph in Exhibit 18.

(a) Cumulative Number of Journals	(b) Cumulative Number of Articles	(c) Column (a) Divided by 326	(d) Column (b) Divided by 1332	(e) Common Log of Column (c)
1	93	0.0031	0.0698	−2.51
2	179	0.0061	0.1344	−2.21
3	235	0.0092	0.1764	−2.04
4	283	0.0123	0.2125	−1.91
5	329	0.0153	0.2470	−1.81
6	364	0.0184	0.2733	−1.74
7	392	0.0215	0.2943	−1.67
8	412	0.0245	0.3093	−1.61
9	429	0.0276	0.3221	−1.56
13	493	0.0399	0.3701	−1.40
14	508	0.0429	0.3814	−1.37
19	578	0.0583	0.4339	−1.23
20	590	0.0613	0.4429	−1.21
22	612	0.0675	0.4595	−1.17
27	662	0.0828	0.4970	−1.08
30	689	0.0920	0.5173	−1.04
38	753	0.1166	0.5653	−0.93
45	802	0.1380	0.6021	−0.86
56	868	0.1718	0.6517	−0.77
68	928	0.2086	0.6967	−0.68
85	996	0.2607	0.7477	−0.58
108	1065	0.3313	0.7995	−0.48
157	1163	0.4816	0.8731	−0.32
326	1332	1.0000	1.0000	0.00

In the third *sample reference*, Brooks (1990) compares cole slope and bibliograph slope (**slope, bibliograph**) for the same data.

Social Sciences Citation Index®. A publication of the Institute for Scientific Information. In its citation index it indicates who cites whom, and so it is often a source of data for a citation analysis in the social sciences.

sociology of science. *See* **science, sociology of**.

EXHIBIT 18.
A curve based on the data in Exhibit 17.
Its straightest part has a slope of 0.47.

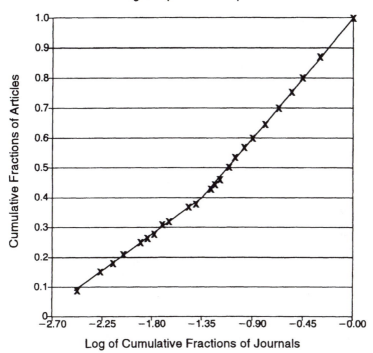

soft science. *See* science, hard and soft.

source document. One of the documents being studied during a bibliometric, informetric, or scientometric analysis. Often the source documents come from a particular subject field and have been published during a specific time period. They may be all the documents that meet these and other criteria, or they may be a sample taken from the population of documents that meet the criteria.

sources and items. *See* items and sources.

speed, citation. *See* mean response time; response time.

standing. A measure of the relative importance or influence of one journal among a group of journals in a given subject area. The basic evidence of standing is how often articles in the journal cite and are cited. Compare with **impact, importance index, influence weight**. Also called **relative standing**.

One who calculates standing is usually analyzing a group of journals by collecting data on how often they cite each other. The data is put into a citation matrix.

In the first *sample reference*, Doreian (1988) explains how the measure of standing may be an improvement over such measures as impact.

In the second *sample reference*, Kim (1992, p. 82) calculates the standing for nine library and information science journals. The standing from journal A to journal B during a given time period is the following ratio:

$$\frac{\text{the number of citaitons from journal A to journal B}}{\begin{array}{c}\text{the number of citations to journal B from all}\\\text{the journals in the group being analyzed}\\\text{plus}\\\text{the number of citations from journal B to all}\\\text{the journals in the group being analyzed}\end{array}}$$

For example, assume the analysis involves three journals that produce the citation matrix in Exhibit 19.

Then the standing from journal A to journal B is:

$$\frac{8}{22 + 12} = 0.235$$

In a complete analysis, the standing of one journal may be expressed as an average of the measures of standing of the journal with each of the others.

statistical bibliography. A prior name for the field of bibliometrics. It goes back at least to E. Wyndham Hulme in the early 1920s and lasted at least into the late 1960s, when Alan Pritchard suggested bibliometrics as a more appropriate term.

The first *sample reference* is a review of two of Hulme's lectures, which together are called *Statistical bibliography in relation to the*

EXHIBIT 19.
A citation matrix for calculating journal standing.

Citing Journals

		<u>A</u>	<u>B</u>	<u>C</u>	<u>Total</u>
	<u>A</u>	15	7	20	42
Cited					
	<u>B</u>	8	2	12	22
Journals					
	<u>C</u>	7	3	5	15
	<u>Total</u>	30	12	37	79

growth of modern civilization. The reviewer notes that Hulme's material shows the "quantitative output of scientific literature in the years 1901-13, and . . . the increase in the number of patents taken out in the past four hundred years" ("Reviews," 1923, p. 173). According to the second *sample reference*, Hulme was a librarian at the patent office in London (Broadus, 1987).

According to the third *sample reference*:

> Statistical bibliography may be defined as the assembling and interpretation of statistics relating to books and periodicals; it may be used in a variety of situations for an almost unlimited number of measurements. Within the last forty years bibliographical statistics have been collected and explained in several fields of science for these main purposes: to demonstrate historical movements, to determine the national or universal research use of books and journals, and to ascertain in many local situations the general use of books and journals. (Raisig, 1962, p. 450)

In the fourth *sample reference*, Pritchard (1969) says:

> Statistical bibliography . . . shed[s] light on the process of written communication and of the nature and course of development of a discipline (in so far as this is displayed through written communication) by means of counting and analyzing the various facets of written communication. (p. 348)

The fifth *sample reference* uses Pritchard's definition in an introduction to a special journal issue on bibliometrics and scholarly communication (Borgman, 1989).

In the sixth *sample reference*, Schrader (1984) identifies an early use of a similar term, "statistical analysis" (p. 251).

The seventh *sample reference* is the paper mentioned by the previous sample reference. It is titled: "A Statistical Analysis of the Literature" of comparative anatomy. It analyzes research production in that field from 1550 to 1860 (Cole and Eales, 1917).

straight count. One way to determine how many documents a person has authored. This is an issue when one is analyzing publications with multiple authors (**authorship, multiple**). Also called **senior count, primary count**. Compare with **adjusted count, complete count**.

For an example of the straight count, assume there are four documents with the following authors:

Document 1 is authored by Queen, Jack, and King;
Document 2 is authored by Jack;
Document 3 is authored by King and Queen.
Document 4 is authored by Jack and Jill.

When doing a straight count, the rule is to ignore secondary authors (**author, secondary**). Therefore, in the above list, Queen has one publication (document 1); Jack has two publications (documents 2 and 4); King has one publication (document 3); and Jill has no publications.

How to count publications arises when working with Lotka's law and sometimes in doing a citation analysis.

In the *sample reference*, Lindsey (1980) describes advantages and disadvantages of various ways to count authorship.

success breeds success. *See* **cumulative advantage**; **Matthew effect**.

successive citation. *See* **citation, successive**.

synchronous obsolescence. *See* **obsolescence, synchronous**.

T

tertiary literature. *See* **literature, tertiary**.

textual analysis. A type of content analysis that focuses on the nature, number, and position of characters, words, phrases, sentences, paragraphs, and sections of a document. Textual analysis may also examine the readability index of a document.

threshold. *See* **cocitation threshold**.

time lag, citation. The number of months or years between the publication of a document and the publication of the first item that cites it. Also called **response time** (of the cited document), **citation speed**.

For example, if an article is published in the April, 1994 issue of a journal and is first cited by an article that appears in the September, 1996 issue of the same or some other journal, then the citation time lag between the two dates is:

September, 1996 minus April, 1994 = 2 years, 5 months;
$$= 29 \text{ months;}$$
$$= 2.42 \text{ years.}$$

Compare with indexing time lag (**time lag, indexing**), and publishing time lag (**time lag, publishing**).

In the *sample reference*, Schubert and Glanzel (1986) apply citation time lag (which they call response time) to many articles and then calculate a mean response time for 109 physics journals.

time lag, indexing. The number of months or years between the publication of an article and the publication of an index that refers to the article.

Indexing time lag is usually a measure of how quickly an indexing service indexes materials. So, this measure is often an average of the time lags for many articles. Indexing time lag can be used to compare the efficiency of two indexing services or to compare how one indexing service processes articles from various journals.

For example, the summary of a study of indexing time lag might include data such as the following:

	Journal A	Journal B	Journal C
Index I	7 months	15 months	8 months
Index II	3 months	12 months	7 months

In this example, indexing service I takes longer than service II to publish index information for all three of the journals. This may be because, for example, index II is published more frequently than index I; or index II does not write original abstracts, but index I does; or index II is just more efficient than index I.

In the above example, journal B is indexed relatively slowly, regardless of the index service. A possible reason for this is delay in shipping issues to subscribers and to the indexing service.

time lag, publishing. The number of months or years between the submission or acceptance of a manuscript and its publication. This usually refers to manuscripts submitted to refereed journals.

One can obtain this measure for some scholarly journals by looking at the bottom of the title page of an article. The editor may say something like: "Manuscript submitted April, 1993; revised November, 1993; accepted for publication January, 1994." If the article appears in the November, 1994 issue of the journal, then the publishing time lag is ten months (counting from the date of acceptance) or 19 months (counting from the date of original submittal).

In the first *sample reference*, Budd (1988) reports publishing time lag for 48 library and information science journals.

In the second *sample reference*, Stankus (1990) describes the publishing time lag and other characteristics of journals in cell biology.

title analysis. A measure of the information content of the title of a document. Content may be examined through factors such as the number and nature of words, syllables, and characters in the title. It may also help to see if the words in the title are repeated in the document itself.

In the first *sample reference*, White and Hernandez (1991) use the Danielson and Bryan readability index to test whether titles become more complex as a field matures.

In the second *sample reference*, Ruben (1992) compares title words of articles in two fields to demonstrate an interdisciplinary link between the fields.

Trueswell's 80/20 rule. Eighty percent of the transactions that move items out of an inventory can be accounted for by 20 percent of the items in the inventory. The percentages are approximate. In a library, the inventory consists of the materials available for circulation to patrons, and the transaction is the circulation process. Also called **80/20 rule**.

The law is named for Richard W. Trueswell (b. 1929), originally an industrial engineer, who later applied some of his ideas to library science.

In the first *sample reference*, Trueswell (1969) demonstrates how a small portion of a library's materials satisfy most of the library's requests for information.

In the second *sample reference*, Selth, Koller, and Briscoe (1992) mention Trueswell's work in their report on a use study of serials and monographs in a library.

In the third *sample reference*, Britten (1990) tests the 80/20 rule for an entire library collection as well as for use within individual classes of the Library of Congress Classification system.

type-token ratio. When applied to the analysis of text (**textual analysis**), this is the ratio of the number of different words (called "types") in a text to the number of words (called "tokens") in the text.

In the *sample reference*, Chen and Leimkuhler (1989, p. 45) use the type-token ratio to produce the following formula, which they find is approximately equal to one:

$$\frac{V_t}{t} + \frac{\ln V_t}{\ln t}$$

where:

V_t is the number of different words;
t is the number of words;
ln is the natural logarithm.

U

uncitedness. The situation in which a document does not receive a citation during a given period of time from a given group of other documents. Also called **noncitation**.

Uncitedness is somewhat related to the concept of internal citation (**citation, internal**), in which a well known author or finding is mentioned in a document but no bibliographic data is provided. However, to be uncited usually means that a document has not been cited.

In the *sample reference*, Stern (1990) examines uncitedness in biomedicine.

utility level of citations. *See* **citation utility**.

W

Waring distribution. A probability distribution that can be used to describe patterns of authorship.

In the first *sample reference*, Irwin (1963, p. 29) may be the first to name the distribution for mathematician Edward Waring (1736-1798). In Waring's original form, it was a formula for the expansion of the expression 1/x-a:

$$\frac{1}{x-a} = \frac{1}{x} + \frac{a}{x(x + 1)} + \frac{a(a + 1)}{x(x + 1)(x + 2)} + \cdots$$

For example, if a = 2, then the above expansion means that 1 divided by x-2 can be written as:

$$\frac{1}{x-2} = \frac{1}{x} + \frac{2}{x(x + 1)} + \frac{6}{x(x + 1)(x + 2)} + \cdots$$

From this expression, in the first *sample reference*, Irwin develops a probability distribution that describes numerical patterns in various fields.

In biology, the distribution can describe how many mites carry zero worms each; how many mites have one worm each; and so on.

In library science, the distribution describes how many authors in a field produce one publication each; how many produce two publications each; and so on.

In the second *sample reference*, Braun, Glanzel, and Schubert (1990, p. 38) show "the simplest definition of the Waring distribution":

$P_0 = a/(a+N);$
$P_k = P_{k-1}(N+k-1)/(N+k+a),$

where:

P_0 is the probability that an event occurs zero times;
P_k is the probability that an event occurs k times;

P_{k-1} is the probability that an event occurs k-1 times;
N and a are parameters.

This version of the Waring distribution is interesting because if authorship is thought of as the "event," then this distribution can take into account situations in which a person is the author of zero documents.

So, in the third *sample reference*, two of the writers from the second *sample reference* use another version of the Waring distribution to determine potential authorship:

$$T = N (1 - f_1)/(1 - 2f_1 + f_1/x)$$

where:

T is the publication potential;
N is the number of authors;
f_1 is the fraction of authors with exactly one publication;
x is the average number of papers per author.
(Schubert and Braun, 1992, p. 5)

To use this version of the Waring distribution, collect data on authorship in a given field and perhaps a given geographic area. For example, assume that in a given country and subject area:

1000 authors have written a total of 2200 documents;
400 of these authors have written exactly one document each.

Then,

N   = 1000 authors;
f_1 = 400/1000 authors = 0.4;
x   = 2200/1000 = 2.2 documents per author;
and
T   = 1000 $(1 - 0.4)/(1 - 0.8 + 0.4/2.2)$ =
       $(1000*0.6) / (0.2 + 0.18)$ =
       600 / 0.38 = 1579

Therefore, this application of the Waring distribution suggests that there are 1,579 potential authors in the country who can write on this topic, even though currently only 1,000 of them are authors.
Compare **Lotka's law, Price's law.**

Willis' law. A statement of the direct relationship between the age of a species of plant or animal and the size of the geographic area that it covers. Compare with **Margalef diversity index**. It is named for botanist J. C. Willis (1868-1958).

In the first *sample reference*, Willis (1922) expresses his law as a principle of age and area:

> The area occupied at any given time, in any given country, by any group of allied species at least ten in number, depends chiefly, so long as conditions remain reasonably constant, upon the ages of the species of that group in that country, but may be enormously modified by the presence of barriers such as seas, rivers, mountains, changes of climate from one region to the next, or other ecological boundaries, and the like, also by the action of man, and by other causes. (p. 63)

Willis also expresses this idea in terms of species and genera. In so doing, bibliometricians can see a similarity between Willis' ideas and bibliometric laws such as Bradford's law. In terms of items and sources, the genera are the sources, and the species are the items. Genera produce species in a way that is analogous to journals producing articles.

In an analysis of 1,028 genera of flora in Ceylon, Willis found that many genera (573) produced only one species each. However, there was a small handful of relatively prolific genera that produced many species each (Willis, 1922, p. 195). This is similar to a subject field having only a few journals that produce many articles each.

In the second *sample reference*, Bookstein (1990) notes that Willis' law shares similarities with other informetric laws.

word profile. A description of a document by the content words associated with the document. Sources of the profile include the indexing terms, keywords, or title words associated with a document.

In the *sample reference*, Braam, Moed, and van Raan (1991a) analyze occurrences of the same words in the profiles of two or more documents. This allows calculation of similarity between the documents. The writers then compare these findings to a cocitation cluster map of the documents.

Z

Zipf's law. A well-known bibliometric law concerning the frequency of words in a text. The law is named for philologist George Kingsley Zipf (1902-1950).

From a given text, count how many times each different word occurs. Rank the words so that the most frequently occurring word receives the rank of one. In English language text, this word is often "the," "a," or some other word with little content or meaning. Then, Zipf's law is expressed actually as two laws.

ZIPF'S FIRST LAW

Zipf's first law is sometimes called Zipf's law for words of high frequency. How high is "high" depends on the text being analyzed. In some situations, "high" is defined liberally enough for the first law to be a good description of almost all the words being analyzed. The first law is:

$$r * f = C,$$

where:

r is the rank of the word that occurs f times;
C is a parameter that depends on the text being analyzed.

In the first *sample reference*, Zipf (1949) says that:

> [W]e have found a clearcut correlation between the number of different words in the *Ulysses* [of James Joyce] and the frequency of their usage, in the sense that they approximate the simple equation of an equilateral hyperbola [the formula given above]. . . . (p. 24)

For example, in Zipf's own analyses of text from *Ulysses*, the 10th ranked word occurs 2,653 times, and the 20th ranked word occurs 1,311 times. The product of 10*2653 is 26,530. The product of 20*1311 is 26,220. This value of C (approximately 26,000) is relatively stable, even down to the 1,000th ranked word, which occurs 26 times. The product of 1000*26 = 26,000.

ZIPF'S SECOND LAW

Zipf's second law holds for words with low frequencies. How low is "low" depends on the text being analyzed, but it almost certainly covers words with frequencies of 1, 2, 3, 4, and 5.

In the first *sample reference*, Zipf (1949, p. 32) gives the law as:

$$N(f^2 - 1/4) = C,$$

where:

N is the number of words that each occur f times;
C is a parameter that depends on the text being analyzed.

In the second *sample reference*, Booth (1967, p. 389) expresses Zipf's second law as:

$$\frac{I_n}{I_1} = \frac{3}{4n^2 - 1}$$

where:

I_n is the number of words that occur n times each;
I_1 is the number of words that occur once each.

Some writers simply talk of Zipf's law, rather than his first and second laws. In such cases, they are often referring to the first law only or to the first-plus-second laws.

zone. See **Bradford zone**.

Sample References

Ajiferuke, I. (1991). A probabilistic model for the distribution of authorships. *Journal of the American Society for Information Science, 42*, 279-289.

Alestalo, M. (1992). Changing social responsibilities of the university: The experience of Finland. *Science and Public Policy, 19*, 43-53.

Arvanitis, R. and Chatelin, Y. (1988). National scientific strategies in tropical soil sciences. *Social Studies of Science, 18*, 113-146.

Atkinson, A. B. (1970). On the measurement of inequality. *Journal of Economic Theory, 2*, 244-263.

Barber, B. (1990). *Social studies of science*. New Brunswick, NJ: Transaction.

Beck, M. T. and Gaspar, V. (1991). Scientometric evaluation of the scientific performance at the faculty of natural sciences, Kossouth Lajos University, Debrecen, Hungary. *Scientometrics, 20*, 37-54.

Bensman, S. J. (1985). Journal collection management as a cumulative advantage process. *College & Research Libraries, 46*, 13-29.

Biggs, M. (1990). The impact of peer review on intellectual freedom. *Library Trends, 39*, 145-167.

Bookstein, A. (1990). Informetric distributions, Part I: Unified Overview. *Journal of the American Society for Information Science, 41*, 368-375.

Booth, A. D. (1967). A "law" of occurrences for words of low frequency. *Information and Control, 10*, 386-393.

Borgman, C. L. (1989). Bibliometrics and scholarly communication. *Communication Research, 16*, 583-599.

Borgman, C. L. (Ed.). (1990). *Scholarly communication and bibliometrics*. Newbury Park: Sage.

Braam, R. R., Moed, H. F., and van Raan, A. F. J. (1991a). Mapping of science by combined co-citation and word analysis. I: Structural aspects. *Journal of the American Society for Information Science, 42*, 233-251.

Braam, R. R., Moed, H. F., and van Raan, A. F. J. (1991b). Mapping of science by combined co-citation and word analysis. II: Dynamical aspects. *Journal of the American Society for Information Science, 42*, 252-266.

Bradford, S. C. (1934). Sources of information on specific subjects. *Engineering, 137*, 85-86.

Braun, H-J. (Ed.). (1992). Symposium on "failed innovations." *Social Studies of Science, 22*, 213-406.

Braun, T. and Schubert, A. (1991). The landscape of national performances in the sciences, 1981-1985. *Scientometrics, 20*, 9-17.

Braun, T. and Zsindely, S. (1985). Growth of scientific literature and the Barnaby Rich effect. *Scientometrics, 7*, 529-530.

Braun, T., Glanzel, W., and Schubert, A. (1990). Publication productivity: From frequency distributions to scientometric indicators. *Journal of Information Science, 16*, 37-44.

Bricker, R. (1991). Deriving disciplinary structures: Some new methods, models, and an illustration with accounting. *Journal of the American Society for Information Science, 42*, 27-35.

Britten, W. A. (1990). A use statistic for collection management: The 80/20 rule revisited. *Library Acquisitions: Practice & Theory, 14*, 183-189.

Broad, W. J. (1981). The publishing game: Getting more for less. *Science, 211*, 1137-1139.

Broadus, R. N. (1987). Early approaches to bibliometrics. *Journal of the American Society for Information Science, 38*, 127-129.

Brookes, B. C. (1969). Bradford's law and the bibliography of science. *Nature, 224*, 953-956.

Brookes, B. C. (1977). Theory of the Bradford law. *Journal of Documentation, 33*, 180-209.

Brooks, T. A. (1990). Clustering in comprehensive bibliographies and related literatures. *Journal of the American Society for Information Science, 41*, 183-192.

Budd, J. (1988). Publication in library & information science: The state of the literature. *Library Journal, 113*(14), 125-131.

Budd, J. M. (1991). The literature of academic libraries: An analysis. *College & Research Libraries, 52*, 290-295.

Budd, J. M. and Seavey, C. A. (1990). Characteristics of journal authorship by academic librarians. *College & Research Libraries, 51*, 463-470.

Burnham, J. F., Shearer, B. S., and Wall, J. C. (1992). Combining new technologies for effective collection development: A bibliometric study using CD-ROM and a database management program. *Bulletin of the Medical Library Association, 80*, 150-156.

Cano, V. (1989). Citation behavior: Classification, utility, and location. *Journal of the American Society for Information Science, 40*, 284-290.

Chall, J. S. (1958). *Readability: An appraisal of research and application.* Columbus, OH: Ohio State University.

Chall, J. S. and Conrad, S. S. (1991). *Should textbooks challenge students? The case for easier or harder textbooks.* New York: Teachers College.

Chatelin, Y. and Arvanitis, R. (1992). Representing scientific activity by structural indicators: The case of Cote d'Ivoire 1884-1968. *Scientometrics, 23*, 235-247.

Chen, Y-S. and Leimkuhler, F. F. (1989). A type-token identity in the Simon-Yule model of text. *Journal of the American Society for Information Science, 40*, 45-53.

Chen, Y-S. and Leimkuhler, F. F. (1990). Booth's law of word frequency. *Journal of the American Society for Information Science, 41*, 387-388.

Chernoff, H. (1973). The use of faces to represent points in k-dimensional space graphically. *Journal of the American Statistical Association, 68,* 361-368.

Cole, F. J. and Eales, N. B. (1917). The history of comparative anatomy. Part I.–A statistical analysis of the literature. *Science Progress in the Twentieth Century, 11,* 578-596.

Cole, J. R. and Cole, S. (1972). The Ortega hypothesis. *Science, 178,* 368-375.

Cole, J. R. and Cole, S. (1973). *Social stratification in science.* Chicago: University of Chicago.

Cole, P. F. (1962). A new look at reference scattering. *Journal of Documentation, 18,* 58-64.

Cook, K. L. (1989). Laws of scattering applied to popular music. *Journal of the American Society for Information Science, 40,* 277-283.

Cook, K. L. (1991). [Letter to the editor]. *Journal of the American Society for Information Science, 42,* 113-114.

Crane, D. (1969). Social structure in a group of scientists: A test of the "invisible college " hypothesis. *American Sociological Review, 34,* 335-352.

Crawford, S. (1971). Informal communication among scientists in sleep research. *Journal of the American Society for Information Science, 22,* 301-310.

Cronin, B. (1981). The need for a theory of citing. *Journal of Documentation 37,* 16-24.

Cronin, B., McKenzie, G., and Stiffler, M. (1992). Patterns of acknowledgement. *Journal of Documentation, 48,* 107-122.

Czerwon, H.-J. (1990). Scientometric indicators for a specialty in theoretical high-energy physics: Monte Carlo methods in lattice field theory. *Scientometrics, 18,* 5-20.

Delendick, T. J. (1990). Citation analysis of the literature of systematic botany: A preliminary survey. *Journal of the American Society for Information Science, 41,* 535-543.

Doreian, P. (1988). Measuring the relative standing of disciplinary journals. *Information Processing & Management, 24,* 45-56.

Drott, M. C. and Griffith, B. C. (1978). An empirical examination of Bradford's law and the scattering of scientific literature. *Journal of the American Society for Information Science, 29,* 238-246.

Edge, D. O. and MacLeod, R. M. (1975). Editorial. *Social Studies of Science, 5,* 3-4.

Efthimiadis, E. N. (1990). The growth of the OPAC literature. *Journal of the American Society for Information Science, 41,* 342-347.

Egghe, L. (1988a). Methodological aspects of bibliometrics. *Library Science with a Slant to Documentation, 25,* 179-191.

Egghe, L. (1988b). On the classification of the classical bibliometric laws. *Journal of Documentation, 44,* 53-62.

Egghe, L. (1990a). The duality of informetric systems with applications to the empirical laws. *Journal of Information Science, 16,* 17-27.

Egghe, L. (1990b). A note on different Bradford multipliers. *Journal of the American Society for Information Science, 41,* 204-209.

Egghe, L. and Rousseau, R. (1990). *Introduction to informetrics*. Amsterdam: Elsevier.

Egghe, L. and Rousseau, R. (1991). Transfer principles and a classification of concentration measures. *Journal of the American Society for Information Science, 42,* 479-489.

Elsevier Science Publishers. (1992). [Statement of purpose.] *Scientometrics, 23,* inside front cover of each issue.

Everett, J. E. and Pecotich, A. (1991). A combined loglinear/MDS model for mapping journals by citation analysis. *Journal of the American Society for Information Science, 42,* 405-413.

Fisher, D. A. (1991). Growth of the Endocrine Society journals. *Endocrinology, 129,* 5-7.

Flesch, R. (1974). *The art of readable writing*. New York: Harper & Row.

Freed, M. N., Hess, R. K., and Ryan, J. M. (1989). *The educator's desk reference*. New York: Macmillan.

Frost, C. O. (1979). The use of citations in literary research: A preliminary classification of citation functions. *Library Quarterly, 49,* 399-414.

Garfield, E. (1972). Citation analysis as a tool in journal evaluation. *Science, 178,* 471-479.

Garfield, E. (1986a). Mapping the world of biomedical engineering: Alza lecture (1985). *Annals of Biomedical Engineering, 14,* 97-108.

Garfield, E. (1986b). Which medical journals have the greatest impact? *Annals of Internal Medicine, 105,* 313-320.

Garland, K. (1991). The nature of publications authored by library and information science faculty. *Library & Information Science Research, 13,* 49-60.

Gatten, J. N. (1991). Paradigm restrictions on interdisciplinary research into librarianship. *College & Research Libraries, 52,* 575-584.

Gidez, L. I. (1991). The peer review process: Strengths and weaknesses–a survey of attitudes, perceptions, and expectations. *Serials Librarian, 19*(3/4), 75-85.

Gluck, M. (1990). A review of journal coverage overlap with an extension to the definition of overlap. *Journal of the American Society for Information Science, 41,* 43-60.

Goffman, W. and Warren, K. S. (1969). Dispersion of papers among journals based on a mathematical analysis of two diverse medical literatures. *Nature, 221,* 1205-1209.

Groos, O. V. (1967). Bradford's law and the Keenan-Atherton data. *American Documentation, 18,* 46.

Gunning, R. (1968). *The technique of clear writing*. New York: McGraw-Hill.

Gupta, U. (1990). Obsolescence of physics literature: Exponential decrease of the density of citations to *Physical Review* articles with age. *Journal of the American Society for Information Science, 41,* 282-287.

Harrison, C. (1980). *Readability in the classroom*. Cambridge: Cambridge University.

Heisey, T. M. (1988). Paradigm agreement and literature obsolescence: A comparative study in the literature of the Dead Sea Scrolls. *Journal of Documentation*, *44*, 285-301.

Herubel, J-P. V. M. (1990). *JSAH*: The sociological character of a journal. *Serials Librarian*, *18*(1/2), 1-11.

Herubel, J-P. V. M. (1991). Philosophy dissertation bibliographies and citations in serials evaluation. *Serials Librarian*, *20*(2/3), 65-73.

Hicks, D. and Potter, J. (1991). Sociology of scientific knowledge: A reflexive citation analysis, or science disciplines and disciplining science. *Social Studies of Science*, *21*, 459-501.

Hilgartner, S. (1990). The dominant view of popularization: Conceptual problems, political uses. *Social Studies of Science*, *20*, 519-539.

Hirst, G. (1978). Discipline impact factors: A method for determining core journal lists. *Journal of the American Society for Information Science*, *29*, 171-172.

Hirst, G. and Talent, N. (1977). Computer science journals–An iterated citation analysis. *IEEE Transactions on Professional Communication*, *PC20*, 233-238.

Irwin, J. O. (1963). The place of mathematics in medical and biological statistics. *Journal of the Royal Statistical Society*, *126A*, 1-45.

James, G. (1976). *Mathematics dictionary*. New York: Van Nostrand.

Kazlauskas, E. J., DeYoe, M. F., and Smith, K. R. (1989). A descriptive analysis of the characteristics of the microcomputer periodical literature. *Journal of the American Society for Information Science*, *40*, 262-268.

Keenan, M. (1988). Report on the 1987 membership survey. *Journal of Finance*, *43*, 767-777.

Kelland, J. L. (1990). Biochemistry and environmental biology: A comparative citation analysis. *Library & Information Science Research*, *12*, 103-115.

Kendrick, A. (1991). A comparison of publication output for academic business librarians with and without faculty rank. *Journal of Academic Librarianship*, *17*, 145-147.

Kidd, J. S. (1990). Measuring referencing practices. *Journal of the American Society for Information Science*, *41*, 157-163.

Kilgour, F. G. and Feder, N. L. (1992). Quotations referenced in scholarly monographs. *Journal of the American Society for Information Science*, *43*, 268-270.

Kim, M. T. (1992). A comparison of three measures of journal status: Influence weight, importance index, and measure of standing. *Library & Information Science Research*, *14*, 75-96.

King, J. (1987). A review of bibliometric and other science indicators and their role in research evaluation. *Journal of Information Science*, *13*, 261-276.

Kinnucan, M. T. and Wolfram, D. (1990). Direct comparison of bibliometric models. *Information Processing & Management*, *26*, 777-790.

Kirby, S. R. (1991). Reviewing United States history monographs: A bibliometric survey. *Collection Building*, *11*(2), 13-18.

Kirton, M. (1976). Adaptors and innovators: A description and measure. *Journal of Applied Psychology*, *61*, 622-629.

Kretschmer, H. and Muller, R. (1990). A contribution to the dispute on the Ortega hypothesis: Connection between publication rate and stratification of scientists, tested by various methods. *Scientometrics, 18,* 43-56.

Kurtz, N. R. (1968). Gatekeepers: Agents in acculturation. *Rural Sociology, 33,* 64-70.

Kyvik, S. (1990). Motherhood and scientific productivity. *Social Studies of Science, 20,* 149-160.

Lancaster, F. W. (1977). *Measurement and evaluation of library services.* Washington, DC: Information Resources.

Lancaster, F. W. (1978). *Toward paperless information systems.* New York: Academic Press.

Lancaster, F. W. (1988). *If you want to evaluate your library. . . .* Champaign, IL: University of Illinois.

Lancaster, F. W., Diodato, V., and Li, J. (1988). Identifying the seminal bridge papers of engineering. *Applied Mechanics Reviews, 41,* 297.

Lancaster, F. W., Gondek, V., McCowan, S., and Reese, C. (1991). The relationship between literature scatter and journal accessibility in an academic special library. *Collection Building, 11*(1), 19-22.

Law, J. and Whittaker, J. (1992). Mapping acidification research: A test of the co-word method. *Scientometrics, 23,* 417-461.

Leimkuhler, F. F. (1967). The Bradford distribution. *Journal of Documentation, 23,* 197-207.

Lewin, K. (1947). Group decision and social change. In *Readings in social psychology,* edited by The Society for the Psychological Study of Social Issues, (pp. 330-344). New York: Holt.

Leydesdorff, L. (1991). In search of epistemic networks. *Social Studies of Science, 21,* 75-110.

Lindsey, D. (1980). Production and citation measures in the sociology of science: The problem of multiple authorship. *Social Studies of Science, 10,* 145-162.

Lockett, M. W. and Khawam, Y. J. (1990). Referencing patterns in *C&RL* and *JAL,* 1984-1986: A bibliometric analysis. *Library & Information Science Research, 12,* 281-289.

Long, J. S., McGinnis, R., and Allison, P. D. (1980). The problem of junior-authored papers in constructing citation counts. *Social Studies of Science, 10,* 127-143.

Lotka, A. J. (1926). The frequency distribution of scientific productivity. *Journal of the Washington Academy of Sciences, 16,* 317-323.

Lunin, L. F. and White, H. D. (Eds.). (1990). Perspectives on . . . author cocitation analysis. *Journal of the American Society for Information Science, 41,* 429-468.

MacRoberts, M. H. and MacRoberts, B. R. (1987). Another test of the normative theory of citing. *Journal of the American Society for Information Science, 38,* 305-306.

MacRoberts, M. H. and MacRoberts, B. R. (1989). Problems of citation analysis: A critical review. *Journal of the American Society for Information Science, 40,* 342-349.

Magurran, A. E. (1988). *Ecological diversity and its measurement*. Princeton, NJ: Princeton University.

Margalef, D. R. (1958). Information theory in ecology. *General Systems, 3*, 36-71.

Martin, F. D. (1992). Information interactions between members of science-profession dyads as reflected by journal use: Ichthyology and fisheries biology. *Journal of the American Society for Information Science, 43*, 276-283.

May, K. O. (1966). Quantitative growth of the mathematical literature. *Science, 154*, 1672-1673.

McCain, K. (1990). Mapping authors in intellectual space: A technical overview. *Journal of the American Society for Information Science, 41*, 433-443.

McCain, K. W. (1991a). Communication, competition, and secrecy: The production and dissemination of research-related information in genetics. *Science, Technology, & Human Values, 16*, 491-516.

McCain, K. W. (1991b). Core journal networks and cocitation maps: New bibliometric tools for serials research and management. *Library Quarterly, 61*, 311-336.

McCain, K. W. (1991c). Mapping economics through the journal literature: An experiment in journal cocitation analysis. *Journal of the American Society for Information Science, 42*, 290-296.

McKinin, E. J., Sievert, M., and Collins, B. R. (1991). Currency of full-text medical journals: CCML and MEDIS vs. MEDLINE. *Bulletin of the Medical Library Association, 79*, 282-287.

Meadows, A. J. (1991). Quantitative study of factors affecting the selection and presentation of scientific material to the general public. *Scientometrics, 20*, 113-119.

Meneghini, R. (1992). Brazilian production in biochemistry. The question of international versus domestic publication. *Scientometrics, 23*, 21-30.

Merton, R. K. (1968). The Matthew effect in science. *Science, 159*, 56-63.

Messeri, P. (1988). Age differences in the reception of new scientific theories: The case of plate tectonics theory. *Social Studies of Science, 18*, 91-112.

Metoyer-Duran, C. (1991). Information-seeking behavior of gatekeepers in ethnolinguistic communities: Overview of a taxonomy. *Library & Information Science Research, 13*, 319-346.

Mikhailov, A. I., Chernyi, A. I., and Gilyarevskii, R. S. (1969). Informatics: Its scope and methods. In *On theoretical problems of informatics*, edited by A. I. Mikhailov, (pp. 7-24). Moscow: All-Union Institute for Scientific and Technical Information.

Miles, I. (1988). *Home informatics: Information technology, and the transformation of everyday life*. London: Pinter.

Moline, S. R. (1991). Mathematics journals: Impact factors and cents per thousand characters. *Serials Librarian, 20*(4), 65-71.

Narin, F. (1991). Globalization of research, scholarly information, and patents–ten year trends. *Serials Librarian, 21*(2/3), 33-44.

Nederhof, A. J. and Noyons, E. C. M. (1992). International comparison of departments' research performance in the humanities. *Journal of the American Society for Information Science, 43,* 249-256.

Nicholas, D. and Ritchie, M. (1978). *Literature and bibliometrics.* London: Bingley.

Nicholls, P. T. (1988). Price's square root law: Empirical validity and relation to Lotka's law. *Information Processing & Management, 24,* 469-477.

Nicholls, P. T. (1989). Bibliometric modeling processes and the empirical validity of Lotka's law. *Journal of the American Society for Information Science, 40,* 379-385.

Ortega y Gasset, J. (1957). *The revolt of the masses.* New York: Norton.

Palmer, J. (1991). Scientists and information: II. Personal factors in information behaviour. *Journal of Documentation, 47,* 254-275.

Pao, M. L. (1986). An empirical examination of Lotka's law. *Journal of the American Society for Information Science, 37,* 26-33.

Peritz, B. (1983). A note on "scholarliness" and "impact." *Journal of the American Society for Information Science, 34,* 360-362.

Pesaran, M. H. (1987). Econometrics. In *New Palgrave: A dictionary of economics,* edited by J. Eatwell, M. Milgate and P. Newman, (Vol. 2, pp. 8-22). London: Macmillan.

Pinski, G. and Narin, F. (1976). Citation influence for journal aggregates of scientific publications: Theory with application to the literature of physics. *Information Processing & Management, 12,* 297-312.

Pratt, A. D. (1977). A measure of class concentration in bibliometrics. *Journal of the American Society for Information Science, 28,* 285-292.

Price, D. J. de S. (1963). *Little science, big science.* New York: Columbia University.

Price, D. J. de S. (1965). Networks of scientific papers. *Science, 149,* 510-515.

Price, D. J. de S. (1970). Citation measures of hard science, soft science, technology, and nonscience. In *Communication among scientists and engineers,* edited by C. E. Nelson and D. K. Pollock, (pp. 3-22). Lexington, MA: Heath.

Price, D. J. de S. (1975). *Science since Babylon.* New Haven: Yale University.

Price, D. J. de S. (1976). A general theory of bibliometric and other cumulative advantage processes. *Journal of the American Society for Information Science, 27,* 292-306.

Pritchard, A. (1969). Statistical bibliography or bibliometrics? *Journal of Documentation, 25,* 348-349.

Prytherch, R. (Ed.). (1990). *Harrod's librarians' glossary of terms used in librarianship, documentation and the book crafts and reference book.* Hants, England: Gower.

Qiu, L. (1990). An empirical examination of the existing models for Bradford's law. *Information Processing & Management, 26,* 655-672.

Raisig, L. M. (1962). Statistical bibliography in the health sciences. *Medical Library Association Bulletin, 50,* 450-461.

Rescher, N. (1978). *Scientific progress: A philosophical essay on the economics of research in natural science.* Oxford: Basil Blackwell.

Reser, D. W. and Schuneman, A. P. (1992). The academic library job market: A content analysis comparing public and technical services. *College & Research Libraries, 53*, 49-59.

Reviews. (1923). *Library Association Record, 25*, 173-174.

Ritter, H. (1986). *Dictionary of concepts in history.* New York: Greenwood.

Robinson, M. D. (1991). Applied bibliometrics: Using citation analysis in the journal submission process. *Journal of the American Society for Information Science, 42*, 308-310.

Rogers, S. J. and Hurt, C. S. (1990). How scholarly communication should work in the 21st century. *College & Research Libraries, 51*, 5-6, 8.

Rorick, W. C. (1987). Discometrics: A system for acquiring scores and sound recordings. *Library Journal, 112*(19), 45-47.

Rousseau, J. J. (1913). *The social contract and discourses.* London: Dent.

Rousseau, R. (1990a). A bibliometric study of Nieuwenhuysen's bibliography of microcomputer software for online information and documentation work. *Journal of Information Science, 16*, 45-50.

Rousseau, R. (1990b). Relations between continuous versions of bibliometric laws. *Journal of the American Society for Information Science, 41*, 197-203.

Rousseau, R. (1992). Concentration and diversity of availability and use in information systems: A positive reinforcement model. *Journal of the American Society for Information Science, 43*, 391-395.

Ruben, B. D. (1992). The communication-information relationship in system-theoretic perspective. *Journal of the American Society for Information Science, 43*, 15-27.

Salancik, G. R. (1986). An index of subgroup influence in dependency networks. *Administrative Science Quarterly, 31*, 194-211.

Schrader, A. M. (1983). Toward a theory of library and information science. Doctoral dissertation, Indiana University, Bloomington, IN.

Schrader, A. M. (1984). In search of a name: Information science and its conceptual antecedents. *Library & Information Science Research, 6*, 227-271.

Schrader, A. M. and Beswick, L. (1989). The first five years of *PLQ*, 1979-1984: A bibliometric analysis. *Public Library Quarterly, 9*(2), 3-24.

Schriek, R. (1991). Most-cited U. S. Courts of Appeals cases from 1932 until the late 1980s. *Law Library Journal, 83*, 317-331.

Schubert, A. and Braun, T. (1992). Three scientometric etudes on developing countries as a tribute to Michael Moravcsik. *Scientometrics, 23*, 3-19.

Schubert, A. and Glanzel, W. (1986). Mean response time–A new indicator of journal citation speed with application to physics journals. *Czechoslovak Journal of Physics, 36B*, 121-125.

Schubert, A. and Telcs, A. (1989). Estimation of the publication potential in 50 U.S. states and in the District of Columbia based on the frequency distribution of scientific productivity. *Journal of the American Society for Information Science, 40*, 291-297.

Schwartz, C. A. (1991). Research productivity and publication output: An interdisciplinary analysis. *College & Research Libraries, 52*, 414-424.

Schwartz, C. A. (1992). Research significance: Behavioral patterns and outcome characteristics. *Library Quarterly, 62*, 123-149.

Selth, J., Koller, N., and Briscoe, P. (1992). The use of books within the library. *College & Research Libraries, 53*, 197-205.

Shapiro, F. R. (1992). Origins of bibliometrics, citation indexing, and citation analysis: The neglected legal literature. *Journal of the American Society for Information Science, 43*, 337-339.

Shaw, D. (1989). Readability of documentation for end user searchers. *Online Review, 13*, 3-8.

Shepherd, M. A., Watters, C. R., and Cai, Y. (1990). Transient hypergraphs for citation networks. *Information Processing & Management, 26*, 395-412.

Sichel, H. S. (1992). Note on a strongly unimodal bibliometric size frequency distribution. *Journal of the American Society for Information Science, 43*, 299-303.

Sievert, M. and Haughawout, M. (1989). An editor's influence on citation patterns: A case study of *Elementary School Journal*. *Journal of the American Society for Information Science, 40*, 334-341.

Snizek, W. E., Oehler, K., and Mullins, N. C. (1991). Textual and nontextual characteristics of scientific papers: Neglected science indicators. *Scientometrics, 20*, 25-35.

Snow, B. (1984). Online database coverage of pharmaceutical journals. *Database, 7*(1), 12-26.

Spiegel-Rosing, I. (1977). The study of science, technology and society (SSTS): Recent trends and future challenges. In *Science, technology and society: A cross-disciplinary perspective*, edited by I. Spiegel-Rosing and D. de S. Price, (pp. 7-42). London: Sage.

SSCI Journal Citation Reports. (1988). Philadelphia: Institute for Scientific Information.

Stankus, T. (1990). Competition as a force in the evolution of science journal format and publishing schedules: A case study from cell biology. In *Scientific journals: Improving library collections through analysis of publishing trends*, edited by T. Stankus, (pp. 173-198). New York: The Haworth Press.

Steinke, C. A. (Ed.). (1991). Information seeking and communicating behavior of scientists and engineers. *Science & Technology Libraries, 11*(3), 1-116.

Stern, R. E. (1990). Uncitedness in the biomedical literature. *Journal of the American Society for Information Science, 41*, 193-196.

Stinson, E. R. and Lancaster, F. W. (1987). Synchronous versus diachronous methods in the measurement of obsolescence by citation studies. *Journal of Information Science, 13*, 65-74.

Stolte-Heiskanen, V. (1986). Evaluation of scientific performance on the periphery. *Science and Public Policy, 13*, 83-88.

Swanson, D. R. (1987). Two medical literatures that are logically but not bibliographically connected. *Journal of the American Society for Information Science, 38*, 228-233.

Tagliacozzo, R. (1977). Self-citations in scientific literature. *Journal of Documentation, 33*, 251-265.

Tibbo, H. R. (1992). Abstracting across the disciplines: A content analysis of abstracts from the natural sciences, the social sciences, and the humanities with implications for abstracting standards and online information retrieval. *Library & Information Science Research, 14*, 31-56.

Tierney, J. (1984, October). Paul Erdos is in town. His brain is open. *Science84*, 40-47.

Todorov, R. and Glanzel, W. (1988). Journal citation measures: A concise review. *Journal of Information Science, 14*, 47-56.

Trenchard, P. M. (1992). Hierarchical bibliometry: A new objective measure of individual scientific performance to replace publication counts and to complement citation measures. *Journal of Information Science, 18*, 69-75.

Trueswell, R. W. (1969). Some behavorial [*sic*] patterns of library users: The 80/20 rule. *Wilson Library Bulletin, 43*, 458-459, 461.

van der Heij, D. G., van der Burg, J., Cressie, I. R. C., and Wedel, M. (1990). Comparative analysis of the penetrative capacity of synopses and of full papers unrelated to the synopses published in the same broad-scope agricultural journal. *Journal of Information Science, 16*, 155-164.

Vlachy, J. (1983). Successive citation of 100 physics papers. *Czechoslovak Journal of Physics, 33B*, 1277-1288.

Wallace, D. P. (1986). The relationship between journal productivity and obsolescence. *Journal of the American Society for Information Science, 37*, 136-145.

Wallace, D. P. (1987). A solution in search of a problem: Bibliometrics & libraries. *Library Journal, 112*(8), 43-47.

Warner, A. J. (1991). Quantitative and qualitative assessments of the impact of linguistic theory on information science. *Journal of the American Society for Information Science, 42*, 64-71.

Weedman, J. (1992). Informal and formal channels in boundary-spanning communication. *Journal of the American Society for Information Science, 43*, 257-267.

White, A. (1991). A further exploration of title size and author number. *Journal of the American Society for Information Science, 42*, 384-385.

White, A. and Hernandez, N. R. (1991). Increasing field complexity revealed through article title analysis. *Journal of the American Society for Information Science, 42*, 731-734.

White, H. D. and McCain, K. W. (1989). Bibliometrics. *Annual Review of Information Science and Technology, 24*, 119-186.

Williamson, E. (1989). Authorship characteristics in five selected regional library journals. *Southeastern Librarian, 39*, 47-52.

Williamson, E. and Williamson, J. B. (1989). Multiple authorship in the southeast. *Southeastern Librarian, 39*, 13-15.

Willis, J. C. (1922). *Age and area: A study in geographical distribution and origin of species.* Cambridge, England: Cambridge University.